SWINDON
IN OLD PHOTOGRAPHS

A VIEW OF NEW SWINDON AND ST MARK'S CHURCH, taken from the site of the present-day Deacon Street in 1885. Note the haystacks in the field where Curtis Street is now.

SWINDON
IN OLD PHOTOGRAPHS

COLLECTED BY
THE SWINDON SOCIETY

SUTTON PUBLISHING
Published in collaboration with

Wiltshire County Council
Library & Museum Service

First published in 1988 by
Alan Sutton Publishing Limited, an imprint of
Sutton Publishing Limited · Phoenix Mill · Thrupp · Stroud · Gloucestershire

This revised compilation first published by Sutton Publishing Limited 1997

Revised and updated by David Bedford, Brian Bridgeman and Jean Allen

Cataloguing in Publication Data is available from the British Library.

ISBN 0-7509-1628-1

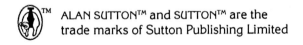
Typesetting and origination by
Sutton Publishing Limited.
Printed in Great Britain by
WBC Limited, Bridgend.

CONTENTS

A VIEW SOUTH ALONG REGENT STREET in the 1920s. The gentleman on the bicycle is taking a risk riding between the tram-lines.

Town Hall and Baptist Tabernacle, Swindon

INTRODUCTION

Until recently, most people thought of Swindon as being a railway town. The Great Western Railway, however, only established its rail works here as late as 1843. Another form of transport, the Wilts and Berks Canal, had previously reached Swindon in 1810 with the North Wilts Canal following in 1819. The former, particularly, was to have a lasting effect on the geography of the town which is still evident today. As the term 'Old Town' still suggests, on the hill overlooking the valley where the canal and railway were to run, there was a community that dated back many centuries. In fact, Swindon was mentioned in the Domesday Book and by the late fourteenth century, when it was known as High Swindon, had some 250 poll-tax payers. It was not a major centre of population, even for that period, and by 1831, not long before the arrival of the railway, its population was only 1,742, still relatively small, the town being considered to be far less important than, for example, Highworth. Times were changing however, and what we now know as the Railway Village was started in 1842 by the GWR as an estate of some 300 cottages for employees of the new works. By the early 1850s the New Town, with a population of almost 2,500, was slightly larger than the old market town on the hill. Over the next fifty years or so the two towns grew together and finally became one municipal borough in 1900, when the total population was 45,000.

The considerable growth of Swindon during this period involves many stories worth recounting. Here are a few of the most interesting . . . . Why, for example, is there a statue of a lion at the junction of Regent Street/Bridge Street and The Parade/Canal Walk? It is popular with young children who like to sit on its back. As the inscription on it clearly shows, it was placed there in 1977 to commemorate the Silver Jubilee of Queen Elizabeth. But why a lion? As the names Canal Walk and Bridge Street suggest, the Wilts and Berks Canal used to flow along what is now Canal Walk and was crossed by a bridge, known as the Golden Lion Bridge. This took its name from the nearby public house of that name, which had a lion standing on a parapet on the roof. For safety reasons the lion was eventually brought down and placed in the forecourt of the public house by the filled-in bed of the canal. When the area was being redeveloped as a shopping area in the early 1960s the Corporation removed the lion for safe keeping. Held in the Corporation yard and put under tarpaulins, it became damp and during the hard winter of 1962–3 froze, later cracking into pieces after surviving many years in the open air. Hence the need for the Council to commission a replacement.

Older residents of Swindon often talk about 'Trip', but what was 'Trip'? It was, in fact, the annual summer holiday for GWR employees and during the first two weeks in July, for as long as the railway was the major employee in the town, Swindon became a ghost town. 'Trip' started as a day excursion in 1849 when 500 people, members of the Mechanics' Institution and their families, travelled in a special train to Oxford. In 1913 the company extended the holiday to a week, but although the trains were free the holiday at that time was unpaid; a fortnight's paid holiday was not introduced until 1946. Trains went to a variety of destinations, but Weymouth was perhaps the most popular resort. In 1934 some 27,000 people travelled on their holidays from Swindon in 30 special 'Trip' trains.

Another form of transport which played an important part in the life of Swindon during the early part of the twentieth century was the tram. At the bottom of what is now the pedestrianised part of Bridge Street, at the junction with Fleet

TRAMCAR NO. 6 at Gorse Hill Terminus, c. 1908.

BARNES TIMBER YARD, Wootton Bassett Road, 1919. Traction engine *Walter Long* used for haulage purposes.

Street, was the Tram Centre. From here trams made their way up Bridge Street, Regent Street and Victoria Hill to The Square in Old Town and back again, with a choice of two destinations from the Centre: Gorse Hill and Rodbourne Road. Victoria Hill may seem a little steep for trams to negotiate and, sadly, so it was on Friday, 1 June 1906, the day of the Great Tram Disaster. The Bath and West Show had opened at Broome Manor Farm the previous day and everyone in the town was eager to make this first visit to Swindon a huge success. Streets and buildings were beflagged and large crowds attended the opening ceremony. Shortly after 7 p.m. on the 1 June, tramcar No. 11 left Wood Street on its return journey to the GWR station. It was raining and the car was packed, with many standing both inside and on the open top deck. Shortly after leaving Wood Street and beginning to travel down Victoria Hill it became obvious that the driver was having problems with the brakes. The tram gathered speed rapidly and began to sway whilst some of the passengers tried to jump clear. One was caught by his coat and dragged along. At the bottom of the hill, on reaching the curve, the car became derailed and turned over on its side. Many of the passengers were injured by the crash and flying glass. The most badly of the injured were rushed to Victoria Hospital by any available vehicle. Four died shortly afterwards and one several weeks later. Thirty others were badly injured, some seriously. One passenger, however, oblivious to all this, tore down Princess Street to catch his train. The Board of Trade enquiry later attributed the cause of the accident to brake failure. Unfortunately, the Corporation was not sufficiently insured against such an accident and the residents of Swindon had to bear an additional rate levy for some years.

Finally, what's in a name? Fleming Way, for instance, or the Lawn area of Old Swindon? Who, or what, were they named after?

Fleming Way, from its junction with Fleet Street, follows the exact course of the old North Wilts Canal, which flowed northwards from a basin outside what is now Debenhams department store, and the Wilts and Berks Canal which flowed east–west from the same basin. Eastwards, Fleming Way follows the track of the canal as far as Drove Road and the Magic Roundabout, passing the abutments of a former canal bridge at York Road. Overlooking the enormous traffic island which marks the end of Fleming Way is the County Ground, home of Swindon Town Football Club, which gives a clue to the origin of the name of the road. Harold Fleming, who played for the Town, won 11 caps representing England between 1909 and 1914.

The Lawn takes its name from the family home of the Goddards, lords of the manor of Swindon for several centuries, which stood in its own grounds to the east of High Street. Twin columns near Charlotte Mews mark the entrance to what was the driveway to the house and the remains of stone balustrades, which border a sunken garden that adjoined the mansion, can still be seen. Nearby are the remains of the Holy Rood which was the parish church of Old Swindon for many centuries.

All the above are illustrated in the following pages, together with many other memories of former years. The new town of Swindon, with its concrete and glass high-rise buildings, prestige office blocks, business parks and an ever quickening pace of life owes nothing to the old working-class railway town, much of which has been swept away in the creation of new shopping centres and offices. Today the population of the newly created 'unitary' Borough of Swindon is 177,700. The final closure of the railway works and redevelopment will soon leave only museum exhibits and the fading memories of older Swindonians to tell a new generation of how life used to be in the old days. We hope that this collection of photographs will bring back memories and stimulate newcomers to the area to learn more of Swindon and its past.

A VIEW OF WOOD STREET AND VICTORIA ROAD JUNCTION from Bath Road c. 1950. To the left, the car park is on the site of the former Congregational Church (see page 71).

The Old Town: Church, Manor and Estate

PROBABLY THE EARLIEST PHOTOGRAPH OF SWINDON. Holy Rood Church, the original parish church of Swindon and first mentioned in documents in 1154. The photograph was taken by Nevil Story-Maskelyne of Bassett Down House in 1847. He was a friend of W.H. Fox-Talbot, who invented negative/positive photography which was patented in 1842. Holy Rood Church was used until the dedication of Christ Church in 1851 and partly demolished the following year. Note the Goddard manor house, The Lawn, to the left of the photograph.

ENTRANCE TO HOLY ROOD CHURCH from Old Mill Lane, 1896.

VICTORIAN CHILDREN in front of the ivy-covered chancel of Holy Rood, 1896.

A GODDARD FAMILY GROUP, c. 1880. Left to right: Ambrose Ayshford (1848–1885), Jessie Henrietta (1850–1920), Ambrose Lethbridge (1819–1898), Charles Frederick (1863–1942), Charlotte (wife of Ambrose Lethbridge, 1824–1904), Edward Hesketh (1855–1921), Fitzroy Pleydell (1852–1927). Ambrose Lethbridge Goddard, lord of the manor of Swindon, was also MP for Cricklade for twenty-seven years. Major/Lieutenant Colonel Ambrose Ayshford Goddard was in the Grenadier Guards and died on board HMS *Tyne* whilst homeward bound from active service at Suakin in the Sudan. He is buried in the Military Cemetery, Valetta, Malta. Fitzroy Pleydell Goddard became the last lord of the manor of Swindon (see page 16). Charles Frederick Goddard later became a clergyman and was Vicar of Clearwell and Rector of Doynton, Gloucestershire. The Christian names of the above appear in the names of various streets, etc., in Old Town. The Goddards were the owners of the manor of Swindon from 1563 and the family resided until 1931 at The Lawn (see page 14).

THE LAWN, west side and Italian sunken garden, c. 1900.

THE GODDARD FAMILY PETS' CEMETERY, in the grounds of The Lawn.

HOUSEMAIDS AT THE LAWN enjoying a few minutes' relaxation from their duties by the fountain in the Italian garden, c. 1926.

THE LAWN, Italian garden and orangery, in the 1920s.

THE LAWN, by now in a sad and dangerously ruinous state, viewed from Old Mill Lane in 1952. Demolished the same year, all that can be seen today of this elegant manor house are the remains of the Italian garden and part of the balustrade wall.

FITZROY PLEYDELL GODDARD, last lord of the manor of Swindon, in 1927. He died later the same year.

HIGH STREET, looking south, c. 1920. To the left is the Goddard Arms Hotel and, on the right, Smith's butchers shop in a building that was formerly the King of Prussia public house.

THE MAIN ENTRANCE TO THE LAWN, High Street, October 1963. The former lodges, situated at the entrance, are in the course of being demolished.

COTTAGES IN LOWER TOWN c. 1910. To the left, over the roof of the lodge on the corner of Old Mill Lane, can be seen the top of the old Methodist Octagonal Chapel (built in 1862 and demolished in 1937) standing behind the Corn Exchange (see *Swindon in Old Photographs: A Second Selection*, p. 74).

LOOKING NORTH TOWARDS HIGH STREET from Lower Town (as this part of Marlborough Road was then called) in April 1908 after a heavy snowfall.

LOWER TOWN (Marlborough Road), looking towards High Street, June 1906. The crowds are coming to the Bath and West Show being held at Broome Farm. To the left is a large stone house, then a veterinary surgeon's premises, now the offices of Cowies of Swindon.

MARKET SQUARE, Old Town, February 1923. To the left is the Corn Exchange (opened in 1866) with its impressive 80ft. clock tower, and the Old Town Hall building (built in 1852) is to the right. The Corn Exchange opened as a roller-skating rink in 1909 and became a cinema in the 1920s. The legend over the door reads, 'Blessed be the Lord who daily loadeth us with benefits'. Today it serves as a bingo hall after being used for ballroom dancing and wrestling promotions. In tramcar days horse-drawn brakes took Swindonians to Coate Water from The Square.

NEWPORT STREET, looking east, c. 1905, when it was lined with ancient whitewashed cottages.

THATCHED COTTAGES in Newport Street and the original 'Old House at Home' c. 1905 (see p. 113).

THE TOP OF CRICKLADE STREET, 1906: the start of the old coach road to Cricklade, which previously had a much more severe gradient, running up to the level of the raised footpath to the left. To the right is the sign of the Lord Raglan, a public house closed the following year (now the site of a new office block). To the left can be seen the premises of Townsends, the solicitors, built in 1729, and one of the most distinguished Georgian town houses in Wiltshire.

NO. 36 CRICKLADE STREET, Old Town, c. 1910.

LITTLE LONDON, Old Town, c. 1912. Formerly known as Back Lane, this is one of the oldest thoroughfares in Swindon and the home of early migrants from London at the beginning of the eighteenth century. Note the steps coming from the back of the Rising Sun public house in Albert Street to the left.

PREMISES OF EDWARD KING, cycle-maker, Albert Street c. 1890.

DROVE ROAD, looking north, in the 1920s. The houses on the left are still in existence.

The Railway Town: Work, Family Life and Leisure

GWR FACTORY WORKERS, L2 (Tank) Shop, 1894.

A FAMILY OCCASION, Emlyn Square, c. 1920. In the background is W.J. Knee's, newsagent and tobacconist shop on the corner with London Street. The Railway Village was built to house workers in the GWR Works.

GWR STATION, c. 1880. This was designed by Messrs J. & C. Rigby of London and opened in 1842.

THE MAIN ENTRANCE, GWR Works, Bristol Street, 1912. Men posing for their photograph to be taken after work. At this time a 54 hour week was worked (of 5½ days) and was arranged as follows:

Breakfast shift 6.00 a.m. – 8.15 a.m.
Morning shift 9.00 a.m. – 1.00 p.m.
Afternoon shift 2.00 p.m. – 5.30 p.m.

On Saturday, the half-day finished at noon. These working hours had dated from 1872 and were not to be reduced until 1919, when a 47 hour week was introduced. In the days of the 54 hour week, the factory steam hooter (see *Swindon in Old Photographs: A Fourth Selection*, pp. 28-9) sounded first at 5.20 a.m. to allow workers from the surrounding villages time to walk to work (the range of the hooter being about 12–15 miles).

GWR MEDICAL FUND HOSPITAL, Faringdon Road, c. 1900. This was opened in 1872 and a 'temporary' extension built onto the garden in 1927. It served the people of Swindon as a hospital until its closure in 1960. The original buildings are now the Central Area Community Centre.

GWR MEDICAL FUND SOCIETY'S consulting rooms, dispensary and swimming baths, Faringdon Road, c. 1900. Erected in 1892, Turkish and other baths were added at the rear in 1899.

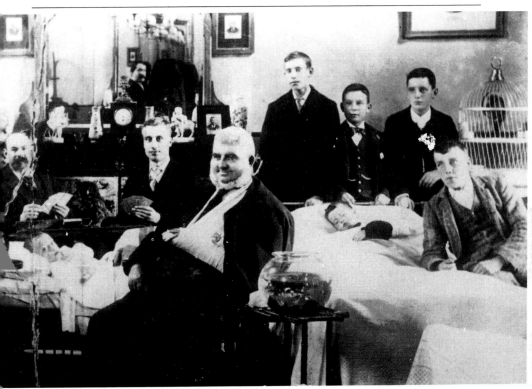

PATIENTS IN THE GWR MEDICAL FUND HOSPITAL, c. 1897. The photographer (Mr Jules Sigismund Guggenheim) can be seen reflected in the mirror. The Great Western Railway Medical Fund Society at Swindon was founded in December 1847, with Archibald Sturrock, Manager of the Works, as President. Among its rules it was stated 'That the object of the Medical Fund is to provide Medicine and Attendance to the men employed in the Works of the Great Western Railway at Swindon and their wives and families'. A subscription was deducted each week by the cashier from every man's wages; it varied from 4d for married men earning more than £1.00 and 1½d for a boy earning less than 10/- (50p). This subscription remained compulsory until the Insurance Act of 1911. The hospital initially had two surgeons, Messrs. Swinhoe and Howse. It was laid down that the hospital was for accidents only and not for general diseases, and was free to all members of the Society.

Mr Guggenheim, the photographer, was in business in County Road between 1891 and 1913.

A VIEW OF NEW SWINDON to the Wesleyan Chapel (now the Railway Museum) in 1885. Note the Wilts and Berks Canal running through the fields in the foreground with the original bridge carrying the track (now Milton Road) over the canal.

WESLEYAN METHODIST CHAPEL, Faringdon Road, C. 1900. Built originally by the GWR as a 'barracks' for single men at the factory, it was extensively rebuilt and consecrated as a chapel in 1869. The building now houses the Railway Museum (opened in 1962).

THE WESLEYAN SCHOOLROOMS AND INSTITUTE, Faringdon Road, c. 1905. A modern office block now stands on this site.

G.W.R. Institute, Swindon

THE GWR MECHANICS' INSTITUTE, opened in 1855, provided many facilities for workers in the factory including a theatre, library, reading and lecture rooms. This photograph dates from c. 1905.

THE OCTAGONAL MARKET, Emlyn Square, c. 1890. It was opened in 1854 to provide meat, fish, fruit and general provisions for GWR employees. Prior to this market being opened, the wives of factory workers had to face the long, muddy trek to Old Town to shop for their families. The building was demolished in the 1890s when the Mechanics' Institute was extended.

THE EXTENSION TO THE GWR MECHANICS' INSTITUTE, Emlyn Square, c. 1900. This was opened in 1893.

READING ROOM OF THE GWR MECHANICS' INSTITUTE, c. 1900. There was always a large range of newspapers and magazines available.

THE THEATRE of the Mechanics' Institute c. 1900.

A VIEW OF THE GWR WORKS from the air, 1920. In the centre of the photograph can be seen the huge 'A' erecting shop, with the Weighbridge House in front. In the background are the terraced streets of Even Swindon/Rodbourne. Newburn House, home of Mr G.J. Churchward, is in the foreground (see p. 35). The Swindon Works of the Great Western Railway in its heyday comprised one of the largest establishments of its kind in the world, covering 326 acres, 77½ of which were roofed, and employed some 12,000 men in many trades in the Locomotive, Carriage and Wagon sections. The Locomotive Department itself comprised some 28 shops and 7,000 men, including pattern makers, foundrymen, smiths, springsmiths, coppersmiths, millwrights, fitters and turners, boilermakers, welders, carpenters, painters and masons.

The Works finally closed in 1986. The offices are now the headquarters of the National Monuments Record Centre while the former Boiler/Machine shops adjacent to Rodbourne Road have recently been converted (March 1997), and opened as the Great Western Designer Outlet Village. Other remaining Works buildings will soon be the home of the Swindon Railway Heritage Museum.

GEORGE JACKSON CHURCHWARD CBE, Locomotive, Carriage and Wagon Superintendent/ Chief Mechanical Engineer from 1902 to 1921, pictured in the lounge of his home, Newburn House, c. 1920. Mr Churchward was killed in 1933 when he was struck by a train while crossing the line near his home one foggy morning. Newburn House was demolished in early 1937.

Churchward was responsible for the design of an entirely new range of locomotives during his period as Locomotive Superintendent which were unsurpassed in performance and efficiency. These included the famous classes such as the 'Cities', 'Saints' and 'Stars', as well as many goods and freight locomotives.

CUTTING AND BAGGING THE CAKE for the GWR Children's Fête, c. 1905. In 1904, 70 cwt. of cake was distributed.

GWR CHILDREN'S FÊTE, c. 1910. This was the great social event of the year in 'railway' Swindon, organised by the Mechanics' Institution from 1868 in GWR Park on the second Saturday in August. In 1904 the crowd numbered 38,000.

GWR CHILDREN'S FETE, The Park, Faringdon Road, 1919 or 1920. Children brought their own mugs on string tied around their necks and received a slab of fruit cake, a cup of tea and one free ride on the roundabouts. The fete was organised by the committee of the Mechanics' Institution and continued annually until the outbreak of the Second World War. A large group of helpers was required to organise such things as the catering, dances, tickets and admissions. Gates opened usually at 1.30 p.m., the admission fee around 1890 was 3d for adults and 2d for children. A spectacular firework display was provided by Wilders as dusk fell. Huge amounts of food were required and large quantities of tea consumed. The roundabouts, with their magnificent horses and steam organs, were very popular and local brass bands also played for the crowds during the day.

THE HORSE-DRAWN GWR PAY WAGON, *en route* to Bristol Street Works entrance, c. 1905. The armoured wagon had been made in the factory and was always heavily escorted.

'TRIP', 1934. Holiday-makers making their way to the GWR station. Note the tramrails of the spur to the station still visible in the road. The tram service was withdrawn in 1929.

'TRIP', 1912. The Mechanics' Institution established the Trip in 1849 for factory workers and their families. In 1905 over 24,000 people left the town, about half of the population, in 22 special trains. Of these numbers travelling, over 5,000 went to Weymouth, 5,000 to the West of England and nearly 4,000 to Weston-Super-Mare. Prior to 1938 the holiday was unpaid and up to 1913 what was termed the 'grand march-past' took place on the following pay-day after the holiday, there being no pay to draw! In 1913 the holiday was altered to mid-week dates so there was at least ½ week's pay to get either side of the holiday.

This photograph, taken by William Hooper, the Swindon photographer, shows Tom Richards, his close friend, leaning out of the window (the second open window from the left).

ST MARK'S CHURCH AND VICARAGE, c. 1880. The church was designed by George Gilbert Scott and consecrated in 1845. Note the gates across Church Road. These marked the boundary between railway property and common ground. Similar gates were placed at other entrances to the Railway Village (see page 28) and were closed on one day a year, restricting access, as a mark of respect for the property of GWR.

WEDDING PARTY outside St Mark's Church, June 1912.

North of the Tracks: Rodbourne and Gorse Hill

RUSH HOUR IN RODBOURNE. GWR workmen leaving the Rodbourne Road entrance to the works c. 1910. Note the tramcar held up in the crowd!

RODBOURNE ROAD, looking north, c. 1905. It is always known as Rodbourne Lane to the locals.

RODBOURNE ROAD TRAMWAY TERMINUS, near Bruce Street, c. 1920.

RODBOURNE ROAD: railway workers at lunchtime c. 1945.

SCHOOL OUTING, Rodbourne Road, c. 1920.

DREW STREET, Rodbourne, in the 1920s. 'A' shop at the GWR Works is in the far distance. This was the most westerly street in Swindon before the western expansion.

THE DOLPHIN PUBLIC HOUSE, Rodbourne Road, c. 1880. In early times the landlord was granted permission to open from 4–6 a.m. on 'Trip' Saturdays for the benefit of early-departing holiday-makers.

THE "DOLPHIN" INN,

EVEN SWINDON.

T. HAYWARD, Proprietor.

The Kingsdown Noted Ales,

Wines & Spirits of First-rate Quality.

CIGARS OF SUPERIOR BRANDS.

A Large NEW ROOM HAS BEEN ADDED,

IN WHICH A

HARMONIC MEETING

Is held EVERY FRIDAY AND SATURDAY EVENINGS,

The Premises possess every Accommodation for holding

Dinners, Bean Feasts, &c., &c.

THERE IS AN EXCELLENT ENCLOSED

QUOIT GROUND AND LAWN ADJOINING

Affording special facilities for unobtruded Enjoyments.

Parties Visiting the Works will find the Inn very conveniently situate, it being almost contiguous to the Rodbourne Lane Entrance to the Works.

ADVERTISEMENT FOR THE DOLPHIN, 1884.

LAYING THE FOUNDATION STONE, Rodbourne Road Primitive Methodist Church, 1900. The cottages to the left are in Rodbourne Road (demolished in the 1960s) and Even Swindon School is to the right. The dignitaries in the front row include: on the extreme right, Mr T.J. Mills, of Mills and Merricks, the local furniture store and, next to him, Mr Levi Lapper Morse and Mrs Morse (see p. 108). The man in the bowler hat directly behind Mr Morse is local builder Mr A. Leighfield and the gentleman beside him, wearing a top hat and with a beard, is possibly the Revd Mr Hunter, a retired minister. The man in the centre of the group, with a bowler hat and a flower in his lapel, may be the Revd Mr Evans, minister at Regent Street Primitive Methodist Church (see p. 73). Third from the left, wearing a Churchill-style box hat is Mr F.W. Vincent, Methodist lay preacher.

THE ORIGINAL GORSE HILL RAILWAY BRIDGE between Cricklade Road and County Road, south side, c. 1890.

LOWERING THE ROAD under the Gorse Hill railway bridge to allow the trams to pass underneath, 1904.

THE ELECTRA PALACE, Cricklade Road, 1913, shortly after opening. This must have been a hot summer! This was the first entirely purpose-built cinema in Swindon. It had 860 seats and a cinema organ. The cinema was well supported for many years, and in 1949 the film *Blue Lagoon* broke all attendance records. The decline of audiences in the late 1950s finally led to closure in May 1959. The building was then used as a motorcycle showroom but later re-opened as the Tatler Cinema, showing adult uncensored films with live striptease on stage! Even this did not pay, however, and it became a Bingo Hall like so many of its counterparts, and has closed recently, a victim of the National Lottery and scratch cards.

ELECTRA PALACE
GORSE HILL   **SWINDON**

A MUTUAL CHAPLIN FILM (2 Reels)

Charlie
Chaplin
In:—THE

COUNT

Thursday, Fri.,
and Sat., Nov. 1
2 and 3

THE STAR DRAMA
WILL BE

THE

VELVET
PAW

Featuring
Gail Kane

Next
Week's
Attractions

MONDAY
5th NOV.

A Sensational Honeymoon
GRAND "IDEAL" PICTURE PLAY

THE GREAT ESSANAY PICTURE REVUE

THURSDAY
8th Nov.

CHASE ME CHARLIE
Featuring **Charlie Chaplin**

POSTER ADVERTISING A FILM at the Electra Palace, 1917.

CRICKLADE ROAD, looking north, c. 1900. On the right Bright Street can be seen.

CRICKLADE ROAD, looking south, c. 1910.

CRICKLADE ROAD, looking south, at the junction with Chapel Street and Ferndale Road, March 1962. To the left, on the corner of Chapel Street, is the original Carpenters Arms public house which was demolished in 1964 for road-widening.

RECREATION GROUND AND GAS WORKS, Gorse Hill, c. 1905.

ST BARNABAS CHURCH, Gorse Hill, c. 1900. The church was consecrated in 1886. In this early view note that the stone wall had not been built around the grounds or the porch built.

ANDERSON'S GROCERS, Cricklade Road (corner of St Paul's Street), Gorse Hill, c. 1905. This is now the Robin's Nest café.

Gorse Hill Schools, Swindon.

GORSE HILL SCHOOLS (opened in 1878), Avening Street, c. 1890.

TRINITY WESLEYAN METHODIST CHURCH, Cricklade Road, c. 1900. The original building on this site dated from 1871, but it was rebuilt and enlarged in 1883 and 1900.

CELEBRATIONS IN CAULFIELD ROAD, Gorse Hill, 1937, for the coronation of King George VI and Queen Elizabeth.

BEATRICE STREET, looking east, c. 1905.

WHITEHOUSE ROAD in the 1950s. Railway workers leaving the Beatrice Street entrance to the works. This area has greatly changed in recent years with the building of Great Western Way and Cockleberry roundabout.

RUSSELL MEMORIAL PRIMITIVE METHODIST CHURCH, Cricklade Road, (corner of Edinburgh Street), c. 1900. Opened in 1890 to replace the building in Chapel Street, it was closed in 1964 and subsequently demolished. Camdale Parade now stands on the site.

THE SALVATION ARMY marching along Chapel Street in 1968 past the former Primitive Methodist Chapel (built in 1871).

Streets, Shops and Industries

REGENT STREET SHOPS c. 1937. 'The Spot' was for many years a Mecca for modellers as well as being a sports shop. 'The Spot' is now the premises of Swiss Chalet.

REGENT STREET, looking south, c. 1905. To the left is the Regent Arcade, an arcade of small shops. To the right is McIlroy's tower, demolished in the 1960s when the shop was modernised.

REGENT STREET, looking south c. 1914. Regent Arcade is now the Arcadia Picture House, which opened in December 1912. It was famous for its 'Childrens' Matinee' or, as it was commonly known, the 'Penny Rush'. The Arcadia later became the Classic Cinema and a bingo hall before demolition. Times Furnishing now stands on the site.

REGENT STREET, looking north, 1913. On the left is the junction with Cromwell Street and the Fox Tavern, the site now being occupied by a corner of Marks & Spencers.

REGENT STREET, looking north, in the 1930s. On the left, Anstiss the drapers, in Swindon until the 1960s and the Arcadia Cinema on the right.

COMMERCIAL ROAD in 1913. This road, with the Market (see pp. 61–63) was named to rival Regent Street, and today has many commercial businesses along its length.

A VIEW SOUTH ALONG BRIDGE STREET AND FLEET STREET from the Tram Centre situated at the junction of these two streets, c. 1912. Note the clock placed in the wall of the shops on the right for the use of the trams. On the left, on the corner of Fleet Street, stands the Oxford Hotel. This was demolished in around 1930 and Burton's the tailors then occupied the site for many years, before it was taken over by Beattie's, toy and model shop.

THE NEW OPEN-AIR MARKET opened in October 1892 in Cromwell Street to replace the old Octagonal Market.

THE MARKET, Cromwell Street, newly covered, 1903. Closed and demolished in 1977, the area was used as a car park for many years until a new market was built on the same site in 1994.

INTERIOR OF THE MARKET around the time of re-opening after being covered in 1903.

SHOPS ON THE CORNER OF THE OLD COVERED MARKET, Commercial Road, 1968.

BARKER'S AERATED WATER MANUFACTORY, College Street, c. 1900. Established in 1879 this was situated near College Street School (see page 83). The building was demolished in 1961.

FEMALE WORKERS IN THE SOUTHERN LAUNDRY, Station Road, c. 1910.

GILLING'S BUTTER FACTORY on County Road/ Station Road corner c. 1905. The building is now occupied by the Kwik-Fit tyre company.

THE FIRST BOTTLED MILK DELIVERIES by New Swindon Industrial Co-operative Society in the 1920s. The photograph was taken in Reading Street.

SWINDON TILE AND POTTERY WORKS, Drove Road. Mr Thomas Turner, proprietor c. 1893. These brickworks provided many of the bricks used in the building of old Swindon and also areas outside the town, including the extension to Marlborough College in the 1880s. Mr Turner lived in Grove House, now the The Grove steakbar/restaurant. He originally, early in the 19th century, had set up business at the Stratton Pottery and Brickyard near the White Hart crossroads at Stratton St Margaret. Turner built three small cottages adjacent to Grove House (see p. 68) which he adorned with many motifs, including pottery pineapples, as a catalogue of pottery available at the nearby works. Amongst these motifs can be seen terracotta plaques showing a bearded face, reputed to be the features of Daniel Lynch, the master potter at the establishment at Stratton. He is said to have pressed his face into damp sand to obtain the first mould. These plaques can be seen on other Turner houses in Turner Street, Westcott Place, Hunt Street, Belle Vue Road, Lansdown Road, Kingshill Road, Avening Street and The Ranger's Centre at Coate Water.

BRICKWORK OF THOMAS TURNER, Hunt Street, 1969.

THOMAS TURNER'S 'CATALOGUE' HOUSE, No. 148 Drove Road, August 1946. This group of houses, fronting the brickyard, was built to show the variety of brick, moulding and terracotta that was available.

LIMMEX, IRONMONGER, at the corner of Wood Street and High Street c. 1905. Note the tramrails in the road.

THE SHOP OF W.J. MORAN, electrical engineer, Victoria Road, 1923, with Mr Moran in the doorway. These premises are now being used by Austin's Leisure Electrical (see also *Swindon in Old Photographs: A Fifth Selection*, p. 52).

INTERIOR OF MORAN'S SHOP, Victoria Road, 1927. Note the period advertisements.

RICHMAN'S, THE GROCERS, Devizes Road, 1921.

NEWPORT STREET, looking east in the 1950s, before road widening. At the end of the street, in Marlborough Road, can be seen the Mason's Arms public house where the Midland Bank building now stands.

Churches, Chapels and Schools

A LOVELY EDWARDIAN VIEW of Swindon with tramcar No. 7 rounding the corner from Bath Road into Victoria Road in 1906. In the background is the Congregational Church, built in 1866 and demolished in 1949. Its site was later used as a car-park before the road was widened in the 1960s.

THE TOWN HALL (built in 1891) and Baptist Tabernacle, c. 1910.

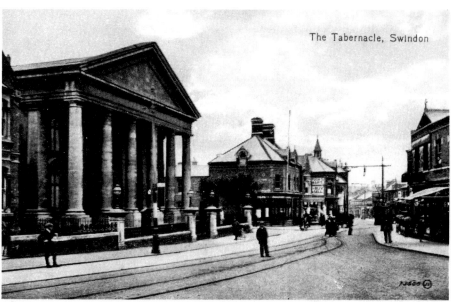

BAPTIST TABERNACLE, Regent Circus, c. 1910, showing its impressive porticoed frontage. Built in 1886, this fine building was demolished in the 1970s.

A VIEW LOOKING NORTH ALONG REGENT STREET from near the Savoy Cinema (now the Savoy bar/restaurant), c. 1945. On the left is the Regent Street Primitive Methodist Church, built in 1876 and demolished in 1957.

THE INTERIOR of Regent Street Primitive Methodist Church c. 1910.

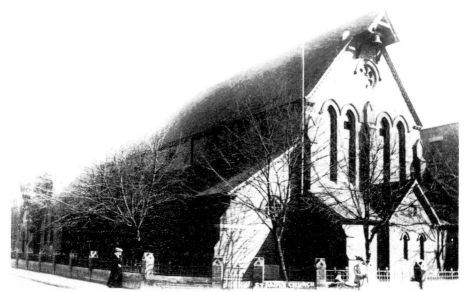

ST PAUL'S CHURCH, Edgeware Road, c. 1905. Consecrated in 1881, it was demolished in 1963. Woolworths store now covers most of the area but a small chapel, St Aldhelm's, was also built on part of the site.

ST PAUL'S SCOUTS, 1914.

LAYING THE FOUNDATION STONE of the Wesleyan Methodist Central Mission Hall, Clarence Street, 1906. As can be seen from the photograph the builders were Tydeman Brothers, Edgeware Road. The architect was W.F. Bird from Midsomer Norton, whilst James Lott of Regent Street were the heating engineers.

METHODIST CENTRAL HALL, Clarence Street, 1971. It was closed in the 1970s and demolished finally in 1985 to make way for a new office block.

WESLEYAN METHODIST CENTRAL HALL, winner of the North Wilts Band of Hope Shield, May 1914.

MR AND MRS LAWRENCE AND DAUGHTERS outside Methodist Central Hall c. 1907. Mr Lawrence was caretaker for several years.

CONGREGATIONAL CHURCH, Sanford Street, opened in 1894 and demolished in the 1970s. A new office block now stands on the site. The date of the photograph is 1968.

BATH ROAD, with the Wesleyan Methodist Church (opened in 1880) on the right, c. 1905.

CHRIST CHURCH, floodlit during the hard winter of 1962–3. It was consecrated in November 1851.

THE CEREMONY FOR LAYING THE FOUNDATION STONE of Christ Church Hall in Devizes Road, 1913. Canon Charles Mayell, vicar of Christ Church, can be seen with other clergy on the platform. In the early years Christ Church Hall was used for overflow services for people who could not get into the parish church.

THE OLD PARISH CHURCH (HOLY ROOD), 3 May 1971, and the first outdoor Whit Sunday service of Old Town Ecumenical Parish. A service has been held on the site of the old church on every Whit Sunday morning since.

INTERIOR OF ST JOHN'S CHURCH, Aylesbury Street, c. 1950. The daughter church of St Mark's, it was opened in 1883, closed in 1958 and demolished soon afterwards. On its site are now the premises of Motolec Ltd.

ST JOHN'S CHURCH: priest, choir and servers. 1943, at about the time of their Diamond Jubilee celebrations. Back row (left to right): K. Cliffe, J. Little, J. McCraken, A. McGovern, D. Wilson, T. Hall, --?--, G. Buss. Second row (left to right): K. Hudson, K. Watts, R. Cutler, D. Davis, C. Cutler, E. Bridgeman. Seated (left to right): Mr Leonard, R. Cliffe, S. Bridgeman, Revd K.C. Davis, F. La Touche, A. Bennett, N. Wilkins. In front (left to right): R. Pearce, D. Woodbridge, J. Keen. D. McGovern, J. Armstrong, B. Watts.

CLARENCE STREET SCHOOL *c.* 1905 (opened in 1897).

MORNING EXERCISES, Euclid Street School *c.* 1910. In 1904 this became a Central Higher Elementary School, one of the first to be opened in the south-west of England.

COLLEGE STREET SCHOOL in early 1961. Built by the GWR in 1873 for the education of infants and daughters of railway employees, it was closed in 1961 and demolished to accommodate the building of The Parade. Stonework bearing the name of the school can still be seen in the passage between College Street and The Parade.

CLASS 7, College Street School, c. 1906.

SWINDON QUARRIES below Lethbridge Road School in 1908 (opened in 1891).

A TRAM CLIMBING VICTORIA HILL C. 1910. To the left is the Technical College, opened in 1895.

Canals, Trams and Motor Transport

A FINE STUDY OF A TRAMCAR at Gorse Hill Terminus around the time of the opening of the service in 1904.

SWINDON NO.1 LOCK, North Wilts Canal, near the GWR Gas Works, Iffley Road and 24 Shop, c. 1880.

WEBB'S WHARF, Albion Street, Wilts and Berks Canal, 1873.

A VIEW LOOKING NORTH TO FLEET STREET SWING BRIDGE over the North Wilts Canal c. 1913. The tram passing over the bridge is advertising the newly-opened Electra Palace Cinema in Gorse Hill.

A VIEW OF THE NORTH WILTS CANAL, looking south from Fleet Street Bridge towards John Street Bridge c. 1913. Fleming Way now lies on the canal bed with the Allied Dunbar building to the left and Alexander House, another office block, on the right.

LOWER EASTCOTT FARM c. 1885, on a corner site which now houses the former Swindon Corporation Electricity Works, Corporation Street.

LAYING RAILS FOR TRAMS, at the junction of Bridge Street and Fleet Street, 1903/4. The gauge of the permanent way was 3ft. 6in.

OPENING DAY OF THE TRAM SERVICE, 22 September 1904, at the junction of Bridge Street and Fleet Street (then known as Clappens Corner). This photograph is one of a series taken that day by William Hooper. See *Swindon in Old Photographs: A Fifth Selection*, p. 97.

TRAMWAY STAFF AT THE DEPOT, 1908. Back row, left to right: A. Brettell, H. Hobbs, F. Neate, - ? -, ?Tunley, C. Chamberlain, G. Nicholls, F. Cull, W. Stroud, W. Reeves. Centre row, left to right: F. Wiltshire, H. Hulbert, J. Cairns, D. Constable, F. Cole, F. Avenell, W. Pagington, C. Simpson, J. Lewis, A. Vizor, ?Alliwell. Front row, left to right: R. Banner, F. Odey, Inspector J. Minto, T. Medcalf (General Manager), Inspector W. Walker, G. Ellery, W. Matthews.

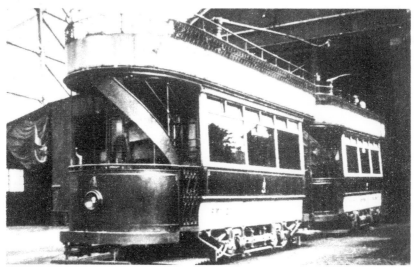

TRAMCARS IN MANCHESTER ROAD DEPOT c. 1905.

A VIEW OF WOOD STREET, looking east and tramcar No. 5. In the distance a second tramcar can be seen at the corner with High Street, c. 1910. During this period it was called Chandlers Corner, owing to the location of Chandler Brothers shop. This is now the site of Boots the chemists.

TRAMCAR IN THE SNOW at the Town Hall on Saturday, 25 April 1908, when 15in. of snow fell on Swindon with drifts up to 6ft. deep. Snow halted the Corn Exchange clock, gutters collapsed and trees split under the weight of snow. Driving an open-fronted tram in such weather was not a pleasant occupation.

GROUP OF TRAMWAY STAFF at Swindon GWR station, c. 1910, seeing off one of their colleagues who was emigrating to Australia.

A TRAM APPROACHING THE CHAINS AND PILLARS OF THE GOLDEN LION BRIDGE over the Wilts and Berks Canal, from Bridge Street c. 1905.

DEMOLITION OF THE GOLDEN LION BRIDGE, July 1918. Built in the GWR Works in 1870, it could be raised to allow canal boats to pass underneath. The photograph shows soldiers constructing the replacement solid embankment. To the left is the Golden Lion public house with the famous golden lion on its parapet on top. (Also see the Introduction.)

LEVELLING BULLENS BRIDGE, over the North Wilts Canal, 1923. A new road (Station Road) is being constructed at canal level just south of the bridge where the filled-in section to the junction begins. The end of the watered section running northwards beneath the railway bridge can just be seen in the foreground.

THE LAST TRAMCAR BODY, No. 13, at Webb's Farm, Chiseldon, 1954. The body had been bought by John Liddiard, a local builder, undertaker and wheelwright, who used it for storage. It remained at Chiseldon until the early 1980s, when it was moved to the Swindon & Cricklade Railway Society's depot at Blunsdon. It is now in storage on a farm near Swindon awaiting possible restoration.

HIGH STREET, looking north c. 1930. One of the first double-decker motor buses, a Leyland Titan with open rear staircase, can be seen turning into Wood Street. These vehicles had been used first in 1929, on the special service provided to and from the Bath and West Show, being held that year off Marlborough Road.

SKURRAY'S GARAGE, High Street, c. 1925.

HIGH STREET, looking north from the junction with Newport Street in the 1950s. To the left is Skurray's Garage.

THE MAIN ENTRANCE TO SKURRAY'S GARAGE, High Street, 1965. The garage was rebuilt in this mock-Tudor style in 1927, demolished in the 1960s and replaced with a contemporary concrete and glass building. When the garage was closed in the 1980s, this was itself demolished and the brick Co-op Superstore built on the site.

SKURRAY'S GARAGE BRAKE-TESTING RAMP, Newport Street, 1935. In the background is the Belmont Brewery owned by Godwin Bros. The main building still stands, complete with chimney, behind the Burmah filling station. Plans are still under consideration to convert the old brewery building to a restaurant and night club.

AN EARLY NEW SWINDON INDUSTRIAL CO-OPERATIVE SOCIETY MOTOR VAN c. 1925.

SWINDON MOTOR ENGINEERING COMPANY, Devizes Road, c. 1932. The building is now FADS Homecare Centre.

Events and People

SWINDON'S FAMOUS TRAM DISASTER, Friday, 1 June 1906. Tramcar No. 11 was repaired in the GWR Works and later returned to service.

FUNERAL of one of the victims of the tram disaster of 1906. The cortège is passing down Kent Road on the way to Radnor Street cemetery.

AN ENLARGEMENT of part of the crowd in County Road in 1897 (see page 101).

QUEEN VICTORIA'S DIAMOND JUBILEE, 1897. Crowds gathered under the decorated arch in County Road, to the south side of Gorse Hill bridge, which can be seen in the background. (See also *Swindon in Old Photographs: A Third Selection*, p. 131).

THE SEWELL FAMILY, relations of the famous writer Richard Jefferies, on Ladder Hill, Marlborough Lane, 1896.

A VICTORIAN FAMILY in the garden of their house in Bath Road, 1896.

MR G. RUSHEN, coachman, in the drive of the house near 'The Brow', Victoria Road, c. 1900.

THE JUNCTION OF HIGH STREET AND WHARF ROAD, Wroughton, on 'Hospital Sunday' c. 1910. In the centre of the group of members of Wroughton Primitive Methodist Band is Bruce, the dog who spent his life collecting for the Hospital Fund in Swindon and the neighbouring villages. With him is his owner, Mr T. Beal of Nelson Street.

SHIELD OF MEDALS AND SILVER COLLAR,
Presented to "BRUCE" for Collecting £700.

BRUCE, wearing his silver collar and medals, presented for services to hospital charities.

CATTLE MARKET AND SHIRE HORSES, Old Town, 1947. Founded in 1254, when Henry III was king, the Cattle Market was moved from the High Street to its site off Marlborough Road in 1887. In the late 1980s the market was closed and a new housing development now stands on the site.

ESTHER 'HETTIE' SWINFORD, a 19-year-old barmaid at The Ship Hotel, Westcott Place, whose murder there in September 1903 by her former fiancé, Edwin Richard Palmer, caused a sensation in Swindon. Palmer surrendered to the police, was tried, found guilty and hanged at Devizes the following November. The *Swindon Advertiser* was brought out in several special editions to report her death and this unfortunate girl's photograph is believed to have been the first ever reproduced in the newspaper.

THE SHIP HOTEL, at the corner of Westcott Place and Birch Street, the scene of the murder of Esther Swinford, in 1902.

'HOOTY', one of Swindon's best-known characters, in the early days of the century. His real name was George French and it is said he received his nick-name by imitating the sound of the GWR factory hooter by blowing down a piece of gas pipe. This old vagabond was also dubbed 'Hooty up the gas pipe' by local children after being found asleep in one of the huge pipes near the old Gas Works in Queen Street. He made his living by making paper windmills on sticks and selling them to children for jam jars which he then sold. Poor 'Hooty' died in poverty in the workhouse in June 1906.

THE CROFT, home of the Morse family who owned Morse's Department Store in Regent Street, during one of the Primitive Methodist Conventions held there from 1903–10. The house was built in 1840 and purchased by Levi Lapper Morse in 1896. Both Levi Lapper Morse and his son, William Ewart Morse, were mayors of Swindon and were also elected as MPs for Wilton and Bridgewater respectively. When W.E. Morse died in 1952, the house and grounds were sold and the site used for the Hesketh Crescent housing estate.

THE ELEGANT DRAWING ROOM of The Croft c. 1910. Note the Moorish-style fireplace.

WEA RAMBLE, C. 1930. In front, extreme right, is Reuben George, who was a much loved and respected local councillor and Mayor of Swindon 1920–21. He was always prepared to fight for the underprivileged throughout his life. When he died in 1936 the townspeople of Swindon ceased work and lined the streets to mourn his passing.

CHARLES GAZE, signwriter, a deeply religious man who always signed his work LJC (Lord Jesus Christ), 1935.

SOME OF MR GAZE'S WORK on the end wall of Hinder's Store, Commercial Road. A new office block, Anglia House, now stands on this site at the junction of Temple Street.

THE REAR OF KEYLOCK'S (BUTCHERS) SHOP, Wood Street, in the 1930s. Mr Keylock's van is decorated for a carnival.

FAIRHOLME, also known as 'Wharf House', Drove Road, c. 1900. This late-Georgian residence was owned by the Gillings family who farmed in what is now the Walcot/Park area and were owners of Gilling's Butter Factory (see page 65). The house was previously the residence of the Wilts & Berks Canal Company's manager and backed on to the canal. It was demolished in 1937 and a garage (now Skurray's) was built on the site.

NEWPORT STREET, October 1954. To the left is the mock-Tudor-style shop 'The Old House at Home', the former National School (rebuilt in 1835) which was Swindon's first school, and the White Hart public house. The latter two buildings were demolished in 1962 when the road was widened, but the lintel, with the name and date of the school, was retained and placed at the side of the new filling station forecourt, but has since disappeared.

A FIRE IN NEWPORT STREET, June 1910. The building, the thatched roof of which caught fire, was the original general stores known as 'The Old House at Home'. On the right is the access road to Swindon Town (MSWJR) station (see also page 21).

CONCERT PARTY IN AID OF THE *TITANIC* RELIEF FUND, outside the GWR Mechanics' Institute, in 1912. Amongst passengers on the liner who lost their lives were two former residents of Swindon, Mr and Mrs Benjamin Howard, late of Cheltenham Street. Mr Howard had worked for the GWR for 39 years before retiring from the Bolt Shop in 1908.

MEET OF THE VALE OF THE WHITE HORSE HOUNDS at The Square, Old Town, c. 1905.

ASTILL'S (PRINTERS) BUILDING, at the corner of Bath Road/Victoria Road, c. 1900. The building was demolished when the road was widened to accommodate the new tramway system in 1904. See *Swindon in Old Photographs: A Second Selection*, p. 18.

ASTILL'S PREMISES decorated for the coronation of King Edward VII in August 1902.

THE FIRST AEROPLANE to visit Swindon, 27 July 1912. M. Salmet, a French aviator, who had been flying all over Britain under the auspices of the *Daily Mail*, landed his aircraft in a field on the Coate Road, near Pipers Corner. Over 30,000 people were gathered there and in adjoining fields. The intrepid pilot performed aerobatics for the excited spectators and in the evening gave a lecture at the Empire Theatre.

'WELCOME SUPPLIES'. The Coal Strike, 6 April 1912; the coal-yard in Coate Road.

COAL STRIKE, Cromwell Street, April 1912. Waiting for supplies at the coal merchants. The National Coal strike, which began on 1 March 1912, brought about a steep reduction in freight business on the railways and reductions to passenger services to conserve fuel stocks.

NO. 5 GLOUCESTER TERRACE (on the site of the present bus station) decorated for the Coronation of King George V and Queen Mary in 1911. In the porch are (left) Harry Brettell; (right) Bert Ponting. At the front are (left) Will Ponting; (right) Jim Ponting.

A DECORATED TRAMCAR for the coronation of King George V and Queen Mary, June 1911, in Manchester Road depot. There were 200 coloured lights on the tramcar.

SWINDON UNEMPLOYED BROTHERHOOD, making toys for Christmas at the Methodist Central Hall, during the Depression 1932.

THE MARKET SQUARE, Old Town, 1935, decorated for the Silver Jubilee of King George V and Queen Mary. In the background can be seen Swindon House, home of Dr Beatty. See *Swindon in Old Photographs: A Third Selection*, pp. 36, 37, 93.

THE JUNCTION OF NEWPORT STREET AND MARLBOROUGH ROAD, believed to have been taken in the 1950s during a royal visit to Swindon. Note the sign for the Mason's Arms hotel yard on the right. Gilbert's furniture store is to the left.

MARLBOROUGH ROAD, 1950s. Crowds gathering to see royal personage. Note, on the right, the lodge on the corner of Old Mill Lane, later demolished for extensions to Green's Garage, itself pulled down in 1987.

GORSE HILL SCHOOL during the coronation celebrations in 1953.

CORONATION PARTY, St Paul's Street, Gorse Hill, 1953.

Swindon at War

TROOPS OF THE 2ND BATTALION, WILTSHIRE REGIMENT, entraining at Swindon Town station, *en route* to Aldershot, 3 August 1901.

THE ROYAL WILTSHIRE YEOMANRY returning from active service in South Africa, 9 July 1901. A civic reception was held at the Town Hall.

THE ROYAL WILTS YEOMANRY, returned from South Africa, *en route* from the GWR station to the Town Hall, in Wellington Street, 9 July 1901.

MEMBERS OF THE WILTS BATTERY AND AMMUNITION COLUMN, 3rd Wessex Brigade of the Royal Field Artillery, arriving at Swindon Town station on 5 August 1914. They are being seen off to war by their families and townsfolk.

THE MAYOR OF SWINDON, Alderman C. Hill, and other local dignitaries bidding farewell to men of the Royal Field Artillery at Swindon Town station, 5 August 1914. Amongst the servicemen was Sgt. William Gosling of Wroughton who won the VC in France in 1917.

MEMBERS OF THE ROYAL FIELD ARTILLERY, in Victoria Road, *en route* to the Drill Hall, August 1914.

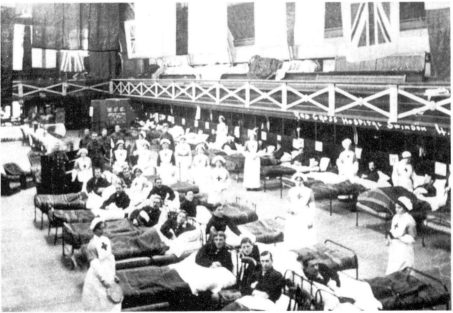

SWIMMING BATHS, Milton Road, during the First World War, while in use as a Red Cross Hospital.

ANZAC TROOPS at the GWR station in World War I.

STANLEY STREET WORKING MEN'S CLUB during World War I. Note the MSWJR timetable and poster, 'Remember Belgium'.

BRAMBLE ROAD POWDER WORKS STAFF, 1917.

EMPIRE THEATRE, March 1916. Wives and children of men in the armed forces attending a free show with refreshments at the theatre through the generosity of 'Raggy' Powell, a local rag-and-bone merchant and philanthropist.

THE EDWARDS FAMILY, Rodbourne, c. 1916. The three serving soldiers all came home unexpectedly. Mother gathered the whole family together and went to the photographers. Her fears for the future could well be imagined but all returned safely.

TRAMWAYS STAFF, 1917. Female conductors replaced many of the men who were serving in the armed forces. This was on the understanding that they would lose their jobs when the war was over.

THE ORIGINAL WOODEN CENOTAPH, which stood near the old Post Office building in Regent Circus, November 1919.

THE NEW CENOTAPH, Regent Circus, c. 1935. This replaced the temporary wooden structure and was unveiled in October 1920.

OFFICERS OF RODBOURNE CHENEY DISTRICT SWINDON HOME GUARD in World War II. Back row (left to right): Mr D. Simms, Mr F. Pryor, Mr Mazzolini, –?–, –?–. Front row (left to right): Mr Smith?, Mr P. Richards, Mr Warminger. The photograph was taken on the rear lawn of Maundrells Farm, opposite the Red Lion public house at Moredon.

BOMB DAMAGE IN FERNDALE ROAD after a raid on 17 August 1942. Bombs fell on Ferndale Road and Kembrey Street and 25 people were killed.

THE INVASION OF SWINDON? No – American troops marching along Wood Street c. 1944.

DROVE ROAD looking south C. 1927. The photograph shows the redevelopment and the first group of new 'semis' completed. The Groundwell Road turning is on the right.

THE SAME HOUSES AS ABOVE, after blast damage, when a bomb fell in Drove Road on 29 August 1942, killing eight people.

SECTION NINE

Leisure and Entertainment

THE RUSTIC BRIDGE in Town Gardens c. 1905. An idyllic view of Edwardian Swindon.

TOWN GARDENS, C. 1910.

SHELTER, Town Gardens, C. 1925.

PARK-KEEPER'S LODGE, Town Gardens, c. 1910.

TOWN GARDENS, c. 1914.

THE BOAT HOUSE, Coate Reservoir c. 1910. Note the early wooden diving board. The reservoir was constructed in 1822 as a feeder for the Wilts and Berks Canal and provided many natural pleasures for our forefathers after long hours of work in the GWR Works.

COATE RESERVOIR, south end, August Bank Holiday, 1911. Photograph by William Hooper's apprentice, Charles Ireland (see page 149).

COATE RESERVOIR, Whit Monday, 27 May 1912.

WOODEN DIVING STAGE, Coate Reservoir, c. 1920.

last old town fair to be held in High Street and The Square, September 1965. This started as a hiring fair in 1216 in the churchyard of Holy Rood. Later, Charles I gave Thomas Goddard, lord of the manor of Swindon, the right to hold fairs twice a year in April and September.

ROLLER SKATING AT THE RINK, The Square, Old Town in 1911. The young girl at the centre of the photograph is Marion Crowdy. She later became a Justice of the Peace for 32 years and was well known in local motoring, legal, girl guide and ceramic circles.

THE GOLDEN LION, a canal-side public house, Bridge Street and a poster advertising a show at the Empire, July 1918.

QUEEN'S THEATRE c. 1905. The new law courts are being built behind the theatre in Clarence Street.

INTERIOR OF QUEEN'S THEATRE c. 1900. The theatre had seating for over 1,000, opened in 1898 and became the Empire in 1906. Serving as a cinema from 1929–47, the theatre closed its doors for the last time in January 1955. It was demolished in 1959, Empire House now standing on the site.

SAFETY CURTAIN, Empire Theatre, 1920s. See also *Swindon in Old Photographs: A Fourth Selection*, pp. 136–37.

ANOTHER VIEW OF BEATRICE STREET LAKE, c. 1910.

BEATRICE STREET LAKE GARDENS c. 1910.

BEATRICE STREET PLEASURE LAKE AND GARDENS, C. 1910. George Whitehead, property speculator, builder and landlord of the Princess Hotel in Beatrice Street, converted an old claypit at the back of the hotel into a pleasure lake in the early years of the century. He charged 1*d*. for admission. The council filled it in during 1973 and the site is now part of St Mark's Recreation Ground.

SWINDON TOWN FC 1912–13. Back row (left to right): Padfield, H. Kay, L.F. Skiller, J. Walker, O.C. Woolford. Middle row (left to right): S. Allen (Secretary), Warman (Asst. Trainer), G. Rushton, W.E.B. Tout, C. Bannister, W.A. Silto, F.B. Handley, Wiltshire (Trainer). Front row (left to right): R.W. Jefferson, H.J. Fleming, F.G. Wheatcroft, J.D. Burkinshaw, A. McCulloch, A.J.W. Bown, S. Lamb, W.T. Bolland.

HAROLD FLEMING. Perhaps the most famous footballer to play for Swindon, he was 'capped' by England in eleven internationals and scored nine goals. He played for Swindon from 1907–24. Harold was a deeply religious man and would not play on Good Friday or Christmas Day. In later years he had a sports shop in Regent Circus. Fleming Way was named after him.

Country Lanes and Outlying Villages

THE WESTERN ENTRANCE TO SWINDON. Wootton Bassett Road under floods c. 1910. In the background is the Running Horse public house.

ST MARY'S CHURCH, Rodbourne Cheney, c. 1905, a medieval church that was so altered during restoration in Victorian times as to be practically a new building. There is a legend that at the time of the Reformation the monks of St Mary's hid a fabulous golden altar somewhere in the network of tunnels said to radiate from beneath the church, but no one has found it yet. . . .

BELLS RETURNED TO ST MARY'S CHURCH after being re-tuned, 1931.

DROVE ROAD, c. 1910. William Hooper, one of Swindon's best-known photographers of the early years of the century, can be seen on his motor cycle, no doubt on another photographic expedition.

TURNPIKE HOUSE, Coate Road, c. 1880. This is the junction of Marlborough Road and Broome Manor Lane as it used to be. Broome Manor Lane can be seen branching off to the right. William Morris (founder of *The Swindon Advertiser*) is seen talking to Mr Skinner, keeper of the turnpike.

PIPER'S CORNER, Coate Road, with Broome Manor Lane branching off to the right, c. 1905.

COATE ROAD, Swindon, looking east, c. 1905. Today a petrol station stands on the site of the cottage to the right.

THE WATER BAILIFF'S COTTAGE, Coate Reservoir, c. 1920. The house still stands and is now the Park Rangers Centre.

THE END OF COATE ROAD, looking east. The bridge over the River Cole is in the foreground, c. 1905.

A THATCHED COTTAGE at Coate with children, c. 1910.

THE SUN INN, Coate, c. 1890, rebuilt in its present form in 1936–7.

LIDDINGTON WICK HOUSE, pictured in 1896. When this photograph was taken, the farm was surrounded by fields. Now the building is part of the Liden housing estate. The farmhouse has now been converted into four flats and has been run by the Thamesdown Housing Association since being purchased in 1978. Several parts of the original Jacobean building remain including a heavily decorated ceiling in one of the flats, very similar in period style to Hangleton Manor at Dovecote, Hove.

The building which was on land once owned by the Duke of Marlborough has had reputedly many uses over the years, including being used as a chapel, and during World War Two it was the local milk collection depot for local farms.

The yew tree pictured still remains, but the front door shown now leads to the boiler house! The heavily studded door was saved and is thought to be in the care of the local museum.

TURNPIKE HOUSE, Wroughton Road, c. 1880. This building still stands, although much altered, in a cul-de-sac near the M4 bridge.

AN EDWARDIAN WEDDING PARTY in the High Street, Wroughton c. 1905.

HIGH STREET, WROUGHTON, looking east, 1908.

LICENSED SLAUGHTERHOUSE AND BUTCHER, High Street, Wroughton c. 1910.

WROUGHTON FC 1908/9. The photograph was taken in front of Wroughton Junior School.

HIGH STREET, WROUGHTON, looking west, c. 1910. The children have been lined up for the photographer.

A VIEW OF CHISELDON, looking north over the railway bridge, in the summer of 1881. Note the windmill, complete with sails, on the skyline. In the late 1980s the structure was taken down brick by brick and rebuilt as a centrepiece of the Windmill Hill Business Park, Wootton Bassett Road, near the M4 motorway.

ELM TREE INN, Chiseldon, c. 1900, when still thatched.

A VIEW TOWARDS THE RAILWAY (MSWJR) at Chiseldon from the slope near the church c. 1900.

A VIEW FROM MOUNT PLEASANT, Chiseldon, over the railway to the church, c. 1905.

CHISELDON, viewed over the railway, with the thatched Elm Tree public house to the left, c. 1905.

ACKNOWLEDGEMENTS

The Swindon Society would like to thank all those listed below for their help in the compilation of this book. Especially Society members Mrs Jean Allen, Denis Bird, Brian Bridgeman and Graham Weare, who undertook the task of putting the book together and selecting the photographs to be used. Also to Denis, Graham and Tony Daglish for providing many photographs from their own collections and Denis again for several from his own camera taken around the streets of Swindon since 1946. The Society would also like to thank all those other members and friends who supplied photographs and information for use and Michael Brougham for the Introduction. Unfortunately only a part of the material available could be used but there is obvious scope for follow-up volumes.

Our thanks also go to Mr Robert Dickinson of the Borough of Thamesdown Museum, Bath Road, for his interest and for allowing us to reproduce several photographs from their collection, to Mr Roger Trayhurn of Swindon Reference Library (Wiltshire Library and Museum Service), the Paragon Laundry, Ridgeway Studios and Mr John Mayhew, Editor of the *Evening Advertiser*.

For individual contributions the Society would like to thank:

Mrs J. Allen • Mr F. Avenell • Mr D. Backhouse • Mr D. Barratt
Mr M. P. Barnsley • Mr A. Barrow • Mr G. Bond • Mr W. Brettell
Mr B. Bridgeman • Mrs J. Bridgeman • Mr R. Clarke • Mrs K. Cook
the late Miss M. F. Crowdy • Mr M. Fox • The Revd F. W. T. Fuller
The Gaze Family • Mr G. Holmes • the late Mrs C. Kilminster • Mr G. E. Lait
Mr J. Lawrence • Mrs B. MacDonald • Mr T. Moran • Mrs S. Povey
Mr P. Sheldon • Mrs M. Sims • Mr M. Smith • Mr R. Stephenson
Mr K. Weeks • Mrs D. Weller • Mr G. Wirdnam.

The Society would welcome any comments or additional information regarding the photographs in this book or in other volumes in the series. Please contact Brian Bridgeman, Publicity Officer, The Swindon Society, 69 Sandringham Road, Swindon, Wiltshire, SN3 1HT.

SWINDON
IN OLD PHOTOGRAPHS
A SECOND SELECTION

A COMPARATIVE STUDY IN CHIMNEYS, 1927. Staff posed in a chimney for the new 'King' Class locomotive *King George V* at the GWR Works with two former types of chimney used on previous locomotives alongside. (GWR)

SWINDON
IN OLD PHOTOGRAPHS
A SECOND SELECTION

COLLECTED BY

THE SWINDON SOCIETY

SUTTON PUBLISHING

First published in 1989 by
Alan Sutton Publishing Limited, an imprint of
Sutton Publishing Limited · Phoenix Mill · Thrupp · Stroud · Gloucestershire

This revised compilation first published by Sutton Publishing Limited 1997

Revised and updated by David Bedford, Brian Bridgeman and Jean Allen

Cataloguing in Publication Data is available from the British Library

ISBN 0-7509-1628-1

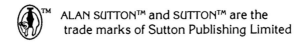

ALAN SUTTON™ and SUTTON™ are the
trade marks of Sutton Publishing Limited

Typesetting and origination by
Sutton Publishing Limited.
Printed in Great Britain by
WBC Limited, Bridgend.

CONTENTS

A VIEW OF THE CROWD at Children's Fête in the GWR Park, 1923. The big social occasion of the year in Railway Swindon was usually held on the second Saturday in August. Only one or two were missed in the First World War and it was to continue up to the outbreak of the Second World War in 1939.

'TRIP', c. 1905. The annual holiday for Swindon GWR workers and their families. Many special trains were provided, positioned both at the station and in many of the Works sidings. A week's pay was lost through 'Trip' until 1913 when mid-week holiday dates provided half pay for two consecutive weeks instead. (Lens of Sutton.)

INTRODUCTION

When looking at modern Swindon today, with its skyscraper office blocks, its dual carriageways and new shopping centres, one remembers what the town was like in that slower age earlier in the century.

There was the 'Old Town Fair', held in the High Street and originally organized as a hiring fair, where farmworkers used to go and present themselves for hire, and farmers from a very wide area would come along and make their choice of labour for a year. It was the excuse for a really happy time and was looked forward to by all, but especially by those who were offering their services for hire. Young labourers, cowmen, etc., would be dressed up in their Sunday best to create a good impression to the farmers, who would, in turn, study each applicant very carefully, knowing that, once hired, they were obliged to keep them, at least until the next hiring fair. Of course, the system died out and the fair as such became unnecessary, but the fun and games associated with it continue until this day, although it no longer obstructs the High Street or Market Square because it interfered too much with modern traffic conditions. It was transferred instead to the County Ground car park.

One remembers the years before the Second World War when the children's (and older folk's) event of the year took place in Faringdon Road Park. Yes, any who were youngsters then will never forget the Children's Fête, an occasion visited by all ages from the cradle to old age, who met for a real day out – free rides on the roundabouts and a ½lb slab of rich fruit cake (supplied by the local Co-op) for the real children, and every sort of entertainment for their fathers and mothers. Side shows, roundabouts, swing-boats, acrobats, dancers, comedians, jugglers, trapeze artists – you name them and they were there. From lunch time until midnight the fun and games went on and there was little peace for folk who lived near The Park, although one never really heard of any complaints. In its early days horse brakes and farm wagons used to pour in from the surrounding district. In later years buses and coaches replaced these slower modes of transport.

At 9.30 p.m. approximately there would be a loud bang and all eyes would turn to the west side of The Park where a hot air balloon could be seen preparing to take off. With a shout from the children 'She's off!', the balloon would rise from the ground and slowly disappear towards the heavens. Ten minutes later another bang would announce a second balloon and, for quite a time, a crowd would gather to watch a spectacular display of fireworks that lasted an hour or so. From coloured rockets to smoke screens in the trees, the crowd would be transfixed as the wonderful splash of coloured fire continued until, at last, the usual set-piece would be lit which said 'Goodnight Children' and, as this died away, there would be a mad rush to catch the public transport home. Long after the time of 'Last cars (trams) and buses' the vehicles could still be seen leaving The Park with overflowing loads of happy but very tired children of all ages, waving flags and clutching balloons on a stick, or sucking lollies and rattling those infernal rattles for which fairgrounds seem to be quite famous. Ah well, another Fête is over, but we'll all be back next year!

Our forefathers also had some very happy times on the old Wilts & Berks Canal. Some will remember sailing down from Gilling's Wharf to Hay Lane on a barge at the annual Sunday School Outing to the raucous strains of 'Pull for the shore,

A TRAMCAR AND A CUSTODIAN OF THE LAW in Faringdon Road, c. 1910. In the background are the Turkish Baths – later a rifle range – in Railway Village.

A TRAM decorated with flags, bunting and coloured lights for Victoria Hospital Carnival Week, 1920s. The photograph was possibly taken in Manchester Road opposite the tram depot.

sailor . . . ', accompanied by a squeaky violin or a creaking mandolin. Alas, the canal became a hindrance to progress and a deposit for all manner of rubbish, so they filled it in. The nearest we can get to those days is a wander along The Parade and Canal Walk, but instead of tree-lined banks, we see on the shore huge stores like British Home Stores and Debenhams. Trams no longer clatter over the Golden Lion Bridge but, on the flyover bridge at Fleming Way, modern buses wait at their central terminus.

Another favourite occasion in old Swindon was the Hospital Shopping Week, when many events were organized with a view to helping the local hospital. The local council used to decorate one of the trams with flags and bunting and outline it with coloured lights, which really was a picture at night. Originally the conductor did not take fares on this tram, but everyone who boarded had to place a coin in the special Hospital box on the platform, and it very often happened that the takings on this car were more than any of the others. In later years, however, when hospitals ceased to rely on charity, the week became known as Carnival Week and ordinary fares were collected in the usual way, but still the decorated car seemed to attract the most passengers.

When recalling the days when the Great Western Railway was the largest employer of labour by far in the area there was one period during the year when the town almost died. This was the annual Trip Week. The first week of July saw a huge exodus of railwaymen and their families as they made for the seaside. All night long, from about nine o'clock on Friday evening until the same time on Saturday morning, folk were making their way to the railway station and the Rodbourne sidings, where many special trains were laid on to places like Weston-super-Mare,

Weymouth, South Wales, Cornwall and Blackpool. Taxis and trams and later buses, also used to run throughout most of the night to accommodate all these eager holidaymakers. The night was quite exciting and the writer has recollections of an obstinate grandfather who, in the pouring rain, always insisted on travelling to the station on the open top deck of a tramcar so that he could smoke his pipe, and of an irate grandmother, struggling up the steps behind, vowing that this would be the last time she was 'coming trip with dad', but she soon forgot and was there again the following year. We never did find out how 'Gramp' used to keep his pipe from going out in the pouring rain!

In the last 'Trip' before the War in 1939 over 27,000 people left Swindon – out of a population of 61,000. Schools and shops closed and Swindon went on holiday. At resorts like Weston-super-Mare, Weymouth and Tenby, the *Evening Advertiser* was always on sale at most newsagents. It was estimated that there were more Swindon folk in Regent Street, Weston-super-Mare, than there were in Regent Street, Swindon, on 'Trip Wednesday', when extra excursions were run for the benefit of the non-Great Western Railway population of the town. Yes, Swindon after the 'trippers' were gone was an empty, lonely, miserable place to be in and it was a great joy to welcome them all back again after the holiday, looking as 'brown as berries' from the sea air and sun.

How Swindon has changed – it seems so long ago that there were so many Sunday afternoon strolls across the fields, yet it is not half a century since one could walk across the fields that are now Pinehurst, to Rodbourne Cheney, to Walcot and across the seven fields to Coate Water, and again along Gipsy Lane and across the fields to Upper Stratton. Sunday afternoon – it requires a long weekend to go in search of the fields now. . . .

Based on *Down Memory Lane*, by Bill Brettell, Swindon Society; some notes and memories of old Swindon.

BRUCE STREET RAILWAY BRIDGE, Rodbourne Road, in December 1955.

High Swindon: Old Town Through the Years

THE LAWN, home of the Goddard family, viewed through trees from the east, April 1908.

11

THE PLANKS, at the rear of the Corn Exchange, the principal route to Holy Rood Church (see *Swindon in Old Photographs*), c. 1910. The raised stone causeway was built for the convenience of churchgoers because the roadway was often flooded in wet weather. The Lawn can be seen in the background.

THE LAWN, viewed from a house in Old Mill Lane, c. 1900.

THE ENTRANCE to the grounds of The Lawn, viewed from the eastern end of Old Mill Lane, April 1908.

COTTAGES IN OLD MILL LANE, C. 1910. Note the pillars to the grounds of The Lawn in the foreground.

A VIEW EAST over Walcot Fields from the grounds of The Lawn in the 1930s. Today all the area in view has been built on.

THE NORTH FACE of The Lawn, c. 1920.

THE LODGE, Old Mill Lane, c. 1910. It was demolished in the late 1960s for extensions to Green's Garage in Marlborough Road.

MARLBOROUGH ROAD, looking north to High Street in September 1953. To the right, Green's Garage and lodge on the corner of Old Mill Lane.

THE LAST THATCHED COTTAGE in Swindon, in Little London, in the 1960s.

THE CASTLE WORKS of Edward Bays & Co., Wood Street, in 1924. The premises later became the Co-op Disco Store but today they are divided into several shops and stores.

KEYLOCK'S, Family Butchers, 17 Wood
Street, 1929/30.

KEYLOCK'S, Family Butchers, Wood Street, delivery van in 1927.

THE CORNER OF VICTORIA ROAD AND BATH ROAD, 1904. Astill's (printers) building (see *Swindon in Old Photographs*) had just been demolished and the corner widened for the new tram service.

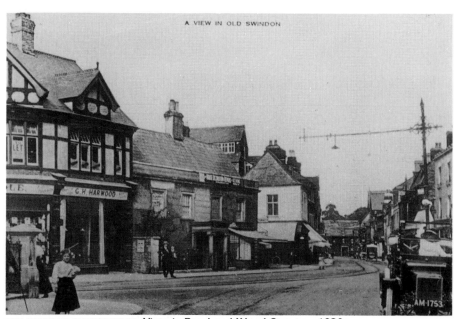

THE JUNCTION OF BATH ROAD, Victoria Road and Wood Street, c. 1920.

THE VIEW looking down Wood Street, c. 1950. To the left is a building known locally as The Manor House. Unfortunately nothing is known of its history. It was demolished in the 1960s and Queen Victoria House now stands on the site.

THE JUNCTION OF WOOD STREET AND BATH ROAD in the 1960s, looking west.

A HOUSE IN PROSPECT PLACE, c. 1900, north of the junction with South Street. These houses were built in the 1830s.

OLIVE HOUSE CHILDREN'S HOME, Prospect Place, c. 1905. For some time this was for girls only, the boys' home being at The Limes, Stratton.

NO. 21 PROSPECT PLACE, on the corner of South Street, c. 1900.

'THE VICTORIA FISH BAR', F.W. Williams' Fish Shop, 52 Prospect Place, 1917. Demolished in 1964.

PROSPECT PLACE, looking from Victoria Road, c. 1960. The former 'Victoria Fish Bar' can be seen to the right, where BBC Wiltshire Sound is today.

F.H. CLARKE, Greengrocer, 64 Devizes Road, after a bus had crashed through the shop window, 1932. The premises are now a sandwich and snack bar called Tuck In.

THE OLD INDEPENDENT CHAPEL in Newport Street. Opened in 1804, this was the first chapel to be built in Swindon. The congregation moved to a new chapel built on the corner of Bath Road and Victoria Street in 1866. The building stood on the north side of Newport Street where the Burmah garage stands today.

DURING THE REDEVELOPMENT OF NEWPORT STREET in 1963/4 the vault under the site of the Old Independent Chapel was discovered after being covered with buildings for many years.

J.B. BRIND, Farrier, Lower Town, c. 1910. The 'top' part of Marlborough Road was formerly known as Lower Town. The building was later demolished but its location was between Nos. 24 and 28 Marlborough Road.

THE TOWER OF THE NORTH WILTSHIRE BREWERY (BOWLY'S), looking west from High Street, c. 1947. The tower was demolished c. 1950. The whole premises have now been redeveloped with only the front wall in High Street remaining. The name 'Bowly Brewer' can still be seen over the archway.

THE TOP OFFICE OF BROWN & PLUMMER, Wine and Spirit Merchants, Market Square, Old Town, 1923. The window to the left is that over the entrance to the bingo hall today.

THE CELLARS AT BROWN & PLUMMER, 1923. These are said to be haunted by the ghost of a former cellarman, Stephen Lawrence, who drowned himself in the church pond.

LADIES had the arduous task of labelling and corking by hand at this time.

THE MARKET SQUARE is honey-combed with underground tunnels, many used by Brown & Plummer Ltd. Here we see rows of barrels, disappearing into the distance, being tapped in the early 1920s.

BOTTLE WASHING at Brown & Plummer, 1923.

LABELLING WINE BOTTLES at Brown & Plummer, 1923.

THE CROFT, home of the Morse family (see also *Swindon in Old Photographs*, pp. 46 and 108), viewed from the south, c. 1910. The gardens of this large house were recognized as having the most picturesque local floral displays in summer. There were also many functions and public fetes held in the grounds. The house was demolished in the 1950s and Hesketh Crescent residential estate was built on the site. Levi Lapper Morse (1853–1913), who purchased the property in 1896, was the founder of Swindon's first departmental store in Regent Street in the 1880s. He was the second Mayor of the Borough of Swindon in 1901/2 and MP for the Wilton division of Wiltshire from 1906 to 1910. His son, William Ewart Morse (1873–1952), also became Mayor of Swindon for two years from 1914 to 1916 and MP for the Bridgewater division of Somerset in 1923/24. He was Vice-President of the Primitive Methodist Church in 1925/26. Winifred Street, built on land adjacent to the Croft, was named after Levi Lapper Morse's wife, Winifred Humphries of Broad Hinton.

THE SWINDON BROTHERHOOD GARDEN FÊTE at The Croft, 19 August 1911. The Morse family, who were closely connected with the Primitive Methodist Church, often opened their home for conventions and other events.

SWINDON SYMPHONY ORCHESTRA at The Croft in the 1920s.

GODDARD AVENUE, looking north, c. 1910. This avenue of fine houses was built on the highest point of Swindon hill around 1900. Named after the Goddard family, lords of the manor of Swindon, it was laid out on land owned by Ambrose Lethbridge Goddard. See *Swindon in Old Photographs*, p 13.

A GARDEN OVERLOOKING TOWN GARDENS in Bath Road, c. 1905.

KINGSHILL CORNER, looking west, c. 1910.

New Swindon: Streets, Shops, Trade and Business

W. & R. FLETCHER, Butchers, 61 Bridge Street, c. 1910. The shop is decorated for Christmas trading.

REGENT STREET, looking north in 1860. At this time it was just a residential thoroughfare with only two or three shops. The roof lines of the houses on the left can still be seen today above the extended shop fronts opposite Woolworths.

A FAMILY GROUP posed in the doorway of their house on the corner of Carlton Street and Wellington Street, c. 1905. The Bus Station now stands on this site.

SKURRAY'S FLOUR MILLS, c. 1900. Built in 1893 alongside the Wilts & Berks Canal near the Whale Bridge. The building remained for many years a part of the garage premises of H.C. Preater Ltd in Princes Street, now Cowies (formerly Walker Jackson's).

THE VIEW WEST along the Wilts & Berks Canal, west of Drove Road Bridge, c. 1913.

THE OLD SKURRAY'S MILL in 1960, shortly before being demolished, viewed from the east towards Whale Bridge.

SARGENT, Blacksmith, 1 Regent Street, c. 1880. Situated at the junction of the Wilts &
Berks Canal and Regent Street and catching the trade from the barge horses. Birthdays, a
greetings cards shop, now stands on this site.

A. E. TUNLEY, artists' supplies shop, 14 Gloucester Street, 1890. It is believed that the gentleman wearing the bowler hat in the centre is Mr Tunley himself. The company still survives today with premises in Fleet Street.

THE VIEW TO THE JUNCTION STATION down Wellington Street, c. 1960. Gloucester Street is to the left. Note Tunley's, still on the corner of Milford Street. All this area is now under the new Bus Station development.

WEYMOUTH STREET from Wellington Street, 1951. The public house on the right is the Mechanics Arms at the junction with Cheltenham Street. All this area was cleared in the 1960s and now lies under the Bus Station. (J. Gould.)

NIBLETT & COMPANY, Aerated Table Water Manufacturers, 20 Cheltenham Street, 1890. Originating in Cheltenham, the company had established a branch in Swindon in the early 1880s. Nibletts later moved to Lagos Street and had ceased trading in Swindon by 1910.

CASH & COMPANY and Dodge Brothers, Boot and Shoe Stores, Fleet Street, c. 1905. Prices range from slippers at 1s. 6d. (7½p) to men's boots at about 5s. 6d. (27½p) a pair. The Central Cinema later took this site in Fleet Street, where Millett's shop is now.

GILLING AND JAMES, Grocers, Milford Street, c. 1905. Note the Gilling Creamery milk cart to the right. The Gilling family also had a butter factory in Station Road. See *Swindon in Old Photographs*, p. 65.

NASH'S SWEET SHOP, 167 Rodbourne Road, c. 1916. Mr Nash, a confectioner, opened his first sweet shop in Regent Circus in the 1850s and opened other shops in the town for each of his daughters. The Rodbourne Road shop sold ice cream throughout the Second World War, which was almost unobtainable elsewhere. It was owned by Mr Nash's daughter Lily and his granddaughter Doris until it closed in the 1970s.

REGENT STREET, 1912. Tramcar No. 2 is travelling northwards on a crossing loop, bound for the Tram Centre. On the right is Fox Tavern, on the corner of Cromwell Street. This was rebuilt in 1913 and finally closed in November 1963. The site now comprises part of Marks & Spencer's store.

MARKS & SPENCER LONDON PENNY BAZAAR, 90 Regent Street, 1911. One of the first open plan self-service shops in Swindon.

COTTELL BROTHERS, Jewellers, 26 Regent Street, c. 1910, with their horse-drawn delivery van outside. Ernest Jones, also jewellers, now occupies the same site next to Woolworths.

MCILROY'S CLOCK TOWER, Regent Street. The clock tower remained in position until the refurbishment of the store in the early 1960s.

F. SPARKES, Family Butcher, 47 Regent Street, c. 1910. The occasion was a window dressing competition.

FLEET STREET, looking east towards Milford Street, with the YMCA headquarters to the left, c. 1904.

THE RIFLEMANS HOTEL, Regent Street, c. 1910.

THE RIFLEMAN'S HOTEL, Regent Street, c. 1955. To the left is the ABC Cinema (now the Savoy bar/restaurant).

THE NEW LAW COURTS, Clarence Street, Swindon, c. 1905.

THE VIEW SOUTH, up Milton Road, April 1908.

THE VIEW looking towards the Grapes Inn, Westcott (later Faringdon Road), *c*. 1900.

FARINGDON STREET (now Road), *c*. 1914.

C. COATES, General Stores & Oil Merchant, 100 Commercial Road, c. 1910. Connell's Estate Agents now occupy this site on the corner of Granville Street.

A. HACKER & SONS, Hay, Straw and Corn Merchants, 6 Corporation Street, c. 1910. The site is now part of the premises of George White, motorcycles. The doorway for the hoist can still be seen behind the building.

FRED SELWOOD, Chemist, Milton Road, c. 1935. Mr Selwood was a well-known local musician and played in Winslow's Orchestra (see p. 104).

AFFLECK, Outfitters and Hosiers, 1 Victoria Road, c. 1910. Robi's Balti House now occupies this site.

A TERRACED HOUSE at 5 Florence Street, Gorse Hill, with the front room converted into a general stores, 1932. Jesse Bridgeman, the owner, is seen in the doorway with his son, Stanley. He also took in shoe repairs.

A SALE QUEUE at Anstiss Departmental store, 73/75 Regent Street, in the 1920s. This well-known local store remained in business until the 1960s but suffered two major fires in its latter years, the second of which destroyed the premises completely.

STAFF OF H.A. REEVES & CO., Hair Specialists, 13 Market Street, October 1934. Left to right: N. Herbert, R. Matthews, E. Elliott, E. Bevington, W. Cook, E. Piper, H. Reeves, J. Smith, B. Bond, D. Cheshire, R. Wilkins, J. Clarke, K. Jones and A. Willis.

THE PREMISES OF H.A. REEVES, Gentlemen's Hairdresser, 78 Commercial Road, prior to the railings being removed (see also p. 129).

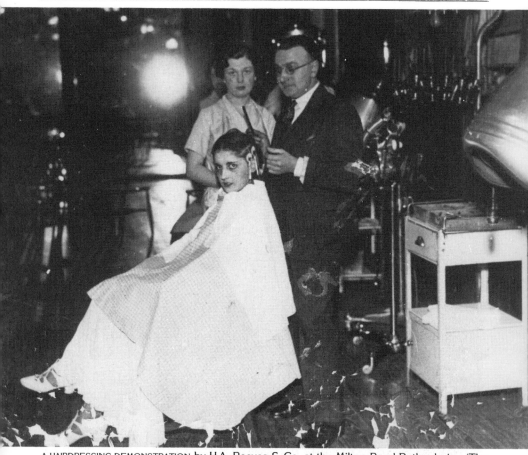

A HAIRDRESSING DEMONSTRATION by H.A. Reeves & Co. at the Milton Road Baths during 'The Better Homes Exhibition' in March 1934. Mr Herbert Reeves can be seen 'perming' the hair of a young model. Standing in the background is assistant, Irene Clarke.

BARRETT & COMPANY, Wholesale Stores/Confectionary and Chocolates, 35 Cromwell Street,
c. 1930. Barretts offered free cinema tickets to their customers.

REGENT STREET, 1945. The façade of these shops has been retained during current redevelopment of this section of the street.

Railways, Trams and Road Transport

THE FAMOUS GWR 4–6–0 express locomotive, *King George V*, while in the USA for 'The Fair of the Iron Horse', the Centenary Exhibition and Pageant of the Baltimore and Ohio Railroad, in the autumn of 1927. In the USA *King George V* was in the care of two Swindon mechanics, chargeman erector F.W. Williams and fitter W. Dando from 'A E' shop, who knew every small detail of this powerful locomotive, under 'Bill' (later Sir William) Stanier. The driver was Mr Young from Old Oak Common, one of the top enginemen of the GWR. This photograph shows the mechanics from Swindon and the footplate men talking to an American female marshall in front of the locomotive during the exhibition. Left to right: Bill Dando, (Driver) Young, (Fireman) Pearce, American lady, Fred Williams. The exhibition was a great success and the Americans greatly admired the simplicity and workmanship of the locomotive.

A SCENE OUTSIDE SWINDON (GWR) JUNCTION STATION, C. 1910, in a more leisurely age when folk still had time to stop and stare. Note the advertisement for Cottells, the Regent Street jewellers (see p. 43).

WAITING FOR A FARE at Queens Hotel cab rank, Station Road, C. 1900. The Queens Hotel (The Tap) is certainly the oldest public house in New Swindon, having its first licence granted in 1841.

THE VIEW EAST from Swindon GWR station in 1906. To the right is Station Road and the Queen's Arms public house (renamed the White House in 1910). (Lens of Sutton.)

THE VIEW NORTH from Rushey Platt signal cabin, near Wootton Bassett Road, in the late 1950s. Today the track bed between Rushey Platt and the Swindon Town station site has been converted for use as a cycle way and footpath.

A GAS LAMP and the original Midland and South Western Junction Railway enamel sign at Swindon Town station, c. 1960. The line closed for passenger services in September 1961.

HOLIDAY CROWDS on the 'down' platform at Swindon Town station, Old Town, in 1928. The line gave direct access to Southampton and the South Coast resorts.

SWINDON TOWN STATION GARDEN and the access road from Newport Street, c. 1947. The station site is now the Central Trading Estate, Signal Way.

SWINDON TOWN STATION GARDEN in full bloom, c. 1947. Relaxing in the sun (left to right) are Bill Morse, John Philpin (Station-master) and Charles Pitman. To the left is the former head office of the M & SWJR, used until recently by the North Wilts Sanitary and Heating Company.

REFRESHMENT ROOMS,
SWINDON TOWN STATION.

TARIFF.

	s	d
Luncheon Basket	3	0
Tea Basket	1	0
Pot Tea	0	6
*Cup Tea	0	3
*Cup Coffee	0	3
Cup Oxo	0	4
Cakes	0	2
Packets of Biscuits	0	2
Chocolates	Usual	Prices
Sandwiches	0	3
Pork Pies	0	5
Glass—Port	0	9
Sherry	0	9
Whiskey	0	9
Brandy	1	0
Rum	0	9
Gin	0	9
Bass	0	8
Worthington	0	8
Guinness	0	8
Bitter	0	4
Cider (per bottle)	0	8
Minerals	0	4

*4d. if taken on Train.

C. D. GODWIN.

TARIFF AT SWINDON TOWN STATION REFRESHMENT ROOMS, c. 1920. The refreshment rooms remained open after passenger services ceased in 1961 and retained their unique Victorian atmosphere, with gas lighting, until final closure in February 1965.

TRAMCAR NO. 6 at Gorse Hill Terminus near Argyle Street, C. 1908.

TRAM CENTRE, at the junction of Bridge Street and Fleet Street, c. 1925.

THE VIEW LOOKING SOUTH up Victoria Hill, with a tram, c. 1925.

MR E.W. STRANGE of Clifton Street, motorman (tram driver) next to tramcar No. 12 at the Gorse Hill Terminus in the 1920s.

SWINDON MOTOR BODY COMPANY, off Station Road, 1923/24. Buses are being built for Bristol Bus Company. Centre of the group to the left of picture is Edwin Bampton, founder of Bampton Bros Coachbuilders, then an apprentice. Lew Webb is the apprentice in the centre of the right hand group. To the left the large house (now demolished) is where Arkell's Mural is today. Houses on the west side of County Road are in the background.

RIME'S GARAGE in April 1924, at the first meeting of the GWR Works Motor Club. In the background are the Law Courts in Clarence Street (see p. 47).

PAGE'S YARD, Page Street, c. 1927. John Page was a local haulier and builder. Originally a cul-de-sac off Princes Street, the street was renamed Beckhampton Street when extended eastwards in the late 1920s.

GREEN AND HARDING GARAGE, Marlborough Road, c. 1930. One of the first Rootes garages, this establishment, as Green's Garage, closed in 1987 and a sheltered housing development has been built on the site.

A CHARABANC OUTING from Ramsbury to Bournemouth, at Salisbury. The Charabanc belonged to the Swindon Charabanc Co. of the Central Garage (Rimes Ltd), who were allowed to display the Swindon Coat-of-arms on their buses. Rimes Ltd continued coach services from Swindon until recent years.

ANOTHER RIMES CHARABANC OUTING, this time to Gough's Caves, Cheddar.

A PICNIC LUNCH in the New Forest for staff of H.A. Reeves, Market Street, August 1935, on an outing to Bournemouth by Rime's coaches.

A LINE UP OF BUSES of 'The Old Firm' at their depot at Spencers Farm, Wroughton, during the Silver Jubilee of King George V and Queen Mary in 1935. 'The Old Firm' was owned and run by the Hawkins family, who lived in the High Street, Wroughton. Father Teddy, sons George, Dennis, Leonard and Ralph, daughters Margery (who kept house), Doris (who drove one of the buses) and Linda (who collected fares). The service ran from Wroughton to Temple Street, Swindon. Ted Hawkins held the carriers licence and ensured that the Swindon Corporation buses could only come as far as the Black Horse public house – the Swindon Borough boundary. As Hawkins were not allowed to pick up passengers from Croft Road or Old Town, the Bristol Omnibus Co. buses were stopped from picking up passengers from Wroughton. The Bristol Omnibus Company took over the route from 'The Old Firm' on 3 July 1955.

A BUS OF 'THE OLD FIRM' at Swindon terminus in Temple Street, C. 1935.

SWINDON CORPORATION Daimler single-deck bus No. 67, pulling away from a Wellington Street halt sign on No. 2 route to Goddard Avenue in 1962. In the background to the right is the entrance to Junction station. To the left is the Railway Mission, used for Christian worship by generations of railwaymen and destroyed by fire in 1979. (P.S.A. Redmond.)

SECTION FOUR

Churches, Chapels and Schools

GORSE HILL GIRLS' SCHOOL, Class IV, 1921. Back row, left to right: G. Weston, I. Coombes, A. Plenty, G. Kirby, -?- Saunders, G. Iles, I. Smith, J. Tavener, K. Sheppard, E. Jordan. Second row, left to right: G. Price, B. Marchant, F. Beckenham, L. Carpenter, A. -?-, E. Weston, M. Herman, C. Wilkins, V. Stevens. Third row, left to right: Miss Winter (Head Teacher) P. Reade, M. Jordan, D. Walton, I. Compton, C. Beale, H. Hall, E. Liton, R. Little, I. Clifford, D. Sellars, E. Wheeler, Mrs Hillier (Teacher). Front row, left to right: L. Turner, L. Savin, L. Beale, M. Titcombe, R. Hayward, J. Lloyd, H. Gardner, C. Turner, L. Dollimore, H. Barkham, J. Hinder.

THE WESLEYAN METHODIST OCTAGONAL CHAPEL, The Planks, c. 1880. Built on the site of a former chapel in 1862 it was used until the opening of a new chapel in Bath Road in 1880. Subsequently it was used by the Salvation Army, then as a stable, a garage and a store until demolished in 1937/8. Until recent years a small piece of arcading, once part of an interior wall could be seen against the wall of an adjoining building before this too was demolished.

THE FAMOUS GWR 4–2–2 broad gauge locomotive, *Lord of the Isles* in front of the newly built St Mark's Church, 1851. This locomotive was displayed at the Great Exhibition of 1851. It was later stored after being withdrawn from service, but was scrapped in 1905.

THE ROMAN CATHOLIC CHURCH, Regent Circus, c. 1900. Built in the 1870s as a Unitarian/Free Christian Church, it was taken over by the Roman Catholics in 1882 and used by them until 1905. Later (1920) it became Swindon's first museum. It was demolished in the early 1930s. Rudi's restaurant now stands on the site.

THE VIEW WEST from Victoria Road to the rear of the Town Hall in the early 1930s. Note the tramrails still in the roadway and the former Roman Catholic Church on the corner to the right. The shop next to it is Affleck's, Men's Outfitter (see p. 50).

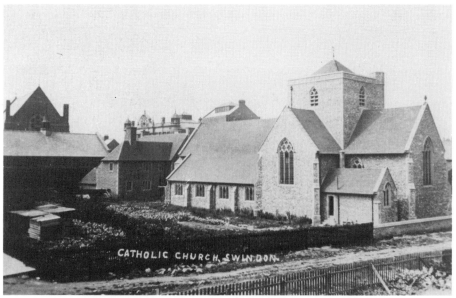

THE NEW ROMAN CATHOLIC CHURCH OF HOLY ROOD, Groundwell Road, c. 1905. A view to the west over what is now Lincoln Street.

Empire Theatre & Presbyterian Church, Swindon.

EMPIRE THEATRE and Trinity Presbyterian Church, Victoria Road, c. 1910. The Empire Theatre was originally called the Queen's Theatre (see *Swindon in Old Photographs*, p. 142) when opened in 1898.

THE INTERIOR OF THE WESLEYAN MISSION HALL, Princes Street, c. 1905, built in 1884 with seating for 240. It was replaced by the Central Mission Hall in Clarence Street in 1907. The building later formed part of Skurray's/Preater's Garage (see p. 142).

CHRIST CHURCH BELLRINGERS, November 1918. The Swindon Parish Church Guild of Ringers rang a special peal of Stedman Triples 5,040 Changes on 23 November 1918 to celebrate the Victory of the Allies in the First World War. Those in the photograph include: H.W. Bishop, A. Lawrence, R.W. Myner, T. Robinson, T. Ricketts, E. Bishop, C.J. Gardiner and A.E.W. Smith.

A 'GOSPEL WAGON', c. 1918. The travelling evangelists were often visiting Swindon and the villages around during these years.

THE BAPTIST TABERNACLE, REGENT CIRCUS, *c.* 1910. Built in 1886 and demolished in the 1970s. The stonework from the impressive frontage was purchased for re-use in a private house in Gloucestershire but it is believed that planning permission was not given.

CROWDS ON THE STEPS of the Baptist Tabernacle during the visit of King George V and Queen Mary to Swindon on 28 April 1924.

BROAD STREET, looking east, 1913. The newly built church of St Luke's can be seen on the left.

FLORENCE STREET MISSION SUNDAY SCHOOL TREAT to Purton in June 1931.

MAY DAY CELEBRATIONS at College Street Girls' School, 1927/28, with an attentive young audience watching through the railings behind the playground, from the site of the former Wilts & Berks Canal. The school was closed in 1961 and demolished to accommodate the building of The Parade shopping centre (see *Swindon in Old Photographs*, p. 83).

CLIFTON STREET BOYS' SCHOOL, Group 9, c. 1907. Note the boy sitting fourth from the right in the second row – a black child would have been most unusual at school in Swindon at this time.

RODBOURNE CHENEY SENIOR SCHOOL, c. 1912. Mr W. Dale, the Schoolmaster, is on the right.

Events and People

BOYS AT THE GWR WORKS who went on strike in June 1915 because their wages were not raised with the men's.

CHARLES BLONDIN (The Great Blondin), the famous acrobat and tight-rope walker, at the Polo Field, Coate Road, *c.* 1890.

THE GREAT FIRE OF REGENT STREET, 10 December 1904. Both the Swindon and the Great Western Fire Brigades rushed to the scene and were able eventually to control the conflagration although the *Swindon Advertiser* reported that there was 'a little unavoidable delay as the Corporation horses usually requisitioned for the fire engines were unfit for work'.

ROSE COTTAGE, 39 Hughes Street, Rodbourne, 1908.

AN EARLY FIRST WORLD WAR TANK on display in Regent Circus, c, 1918. The Head Post Office, on the corner of Princes Street, is in the background.

STAFF OF THE RED CROSS HOSPITAL at the GWR Medical Fund Baths, January 1915.

ALICE EDWARDS outside her home, 32 Thomas Street, Rodbourne, c. 1912. A lovely study of a typical terraced house in GWR Swindon.

A WRECKED AIRCRAFT at Lydiard Tregoze, 10 May 1913. Many of the people of Swindon looked skywards on this Saturday evening to see an aeroplane passing over the town. The pilot lost his way after leaving the town and landed in a field at Lydiard Tregoze. Attempting to take off again the aircraft turned over and was wrecked. Luckily neither of the occupants, an officer from the Flying School at Netheravon and his pupil, were injured.

ANOTHER AEROPLANE ACCIDENT, Thomas Street, Rodbourne. Mrs Leighfield and her daughter with a fragment of aircraft which fell off into their garden. The aircraft was advertising the *Daily Mail, c.* 1924/5.

ARTHUR 'POP' Jarman, left, in Guppy Street, c. 1910, with one of the rickshaws he designed and manufactured. The gentleman on the right is Henry Hacker.

THE TYDEMAN FAMILY in a horse-drawn trap. Edgeware Road, c. 1910. The Tydeman Brothers were a well-known firm of local builders for many years.

STAFF of the Old Swindon and New Swindon branches of The Capital and Counties Bank Limited, 1894. Standing, left to right: F.S. Wilson, C. Sneath, E.J. Badcock, H.C. Cook. Seated, left to right: H.T. Dixon, E. Ing, T. Byrch, C.R. Bailey, H. Rivers. In front: D.C. Waddy.

FLOODS IN CROMWELL STREET, 22 July 1922. For many years this part of New Swindon often flooded after heavy thunderstorms until drainage was improved.

FLOODS IN CROMWELL STREET, 11 July 1927.

SWINDON CARNIVAL QUEEN AND ATTENDANTS, 1936. Left to right: Madge Bridges, Jessie Cullingford, Joyce Gooding (Queen), Dulcie Seager, Gwenda Binks. Gwenda Binks is the mother of Justin Hayward, the singer/guitarist with the Moody Blues and of *Nights in White Satin* fame.

SWINDON CARNIVAL QUEEN and attendants in 1939. Left to right: Rose Ward, Glenys Williams, Olive Browning (Queen), Doris Taylor and Margaret Kitching.

NELLIE EMILY LYDIA BEESLEY in the garden of 66 Curtis Street, c. 1920. J.B. Beesley was Swindon's first wholesale fruiterer.

PERCY WILLIAMS of Theobald Street who, after serving an apprenticeship at the GWR Railway Works, became a sea-going engineer with the Blue Star line. He enlisted in the British Battalion of the International Brigades during the Spanish Civil War and was killed in Spain in March 1938. His memorial in Whitworth Road cemetery was erected in 1939 by the District Committee of the Amalgamated Engineering Union.

SECTION SIX

Sports and
Entertainment

SWINDON ROVERS FOOTBALL CLUB, 1901–2. Back row, left to right: W.J. Davis (Trainer), F.W. Bickel, W. Bayliss (Captain), W.H. Finney, C. Morris, F. Harper, D. Williams (Linesman). Seated, left to right: B. Fryers, C.C. Henry, C.K. Jones, C.C. Champeny, H.R. Plaister. Front row, left to right: A.E. Hopkins, A.V. Plaister, W.R. Hill (Hon Sec & Treasurer).

FOOTBALL ACTION during one of Swindon Town Football Club's matches at the County Ground, c. 1912.

MORE FOOTBALL ACTION at the County Ground in pre-First World War days.

In Memory of Dear Old

Notts County

WHO FELL AT THE

County Ground, Swindon,

FIGHTING FOR THE

ENGLISH CUP,

JANUARY 14TH, 1911.

Three cheers, three cheers for Swindon,
And a groan for men of lace,
Who could not stand the first round
Because of Swindon's pace.
Then away ye sons of Robin Hood!
'tis Swindon's Merry Men
Will march right on to the Cup this time,
Will you come to the Palace then?

Funeral arrangements by the Trainer.

Swindon 3 ; Notts County 1

Maybu 's, Printers, Swindon

SPECIALLY PRINTED 'IN MEMORIUM' CARDS for two of Swindon Town's matches in the FA Cup prior to the First World War, during the Southern League heyday, when the football club reached the semi-final twice in three years.

In Memory of

EVERTON

WHO FELL FIGHTING FOR THE

ENGLISH CUP,
(Fourth Round)

At County Ground, Swindon.

MARCH 9th, 1912.

Team that died in the South,
Fighting so well and hard,
Surely you too have won,
This little Mourning Card.
Sweetly taking your rest,
Sleeping so safe and sound,
Killed by those terrible Robins,
Killed in the fatal Fourth Round.

Swindon 2 Everton 1

Maybury's, Printers, Swindon

THESE LADIES were winners of the Hockey League 1908/09/10.

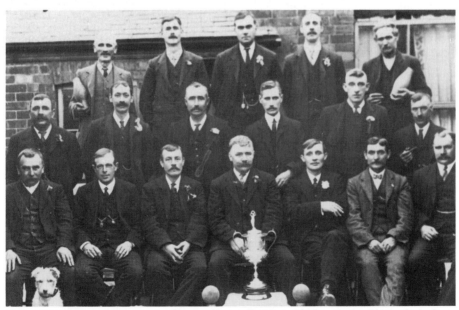

NORTH SWINDON WORKMEN'S CLUB, Cheney Manor Road, c. 1915, with the Skittle Club Cup. Edward Woolford, Captain, is in the centre of the front row.

CHRIST CHURCH FOOTBALL CLUB, 1923/24. The photograph was possibly taken in the garden of the Vicarage in Bath Road.

SWINDON ATHLETIC CLUB one mile relay team, c. 1924. Back row, left to right: A.J. Jones (440 yds), J. Porter (880 yds). Front row, left to right: B.L. Kibblewhite (220 yds), Hewlitt (220 yds).

THE 'NEW' CONCRETE DIVING STAGE at Coate Water, 1935. Designed by the Borough Surveyor in association with the Federation Internationale de Natation Amateur. Unfortunately, pollution of the lake means that no-one now dives from this structure.

THE WATER POLO TEAM at Coate Water in the 1930s.

MOREDON ROYAL OAK CRICKET CLUB, 1901. Back row, left to right: M. House, P. Titcombe, J. Lewis, A.E. Thorne, J. Peaple (Umpire), J. Walters (Sub-Captain). Middle row, left to right: W. Beasant, A. Stroud (Captain), J.H. Maundrell (President), E. Lucas, R. Francome (Secretary). Front row, left to right: J. Bendell, A.E. Hurcom (Scorer), W. Strange.

THE BAND OF THE F & G COMPANIES of a Battalion of the Rifle Volunteers, Wiltshire Regiment, outside the Mechanics Institute, c. 1880.

GWR (SOCIAL AND EDUCATIONAL) BAND, 1928. This photograph was taken on a Sunday morning in front of the Mechanics Institute just after the band had won the *Daily Mirror* Cup (4th Section) at Crystal Palace.

THE "ORIGINAL MOONIES"
GEO. and FRED.

'THE MOONRAKERS OF GOOCH STREET'. A local variety act, George Brooks and Fred James, prior to the First World War.

WINSLOW'S (SWINDON) MANDOLIN ORCHESTRA. A photograph taken at BBC Bristol Studio, May 1935. Back row (left to right): -?-, -?-, -?-, F. Selwood, Mr Llewelyn, Mr Leech, C. Dommett, B. Parker. Front row (left to right): -?-, S. Price, W. Clifford, Fred Winslow (Band Leader), -?-, Mr Costello, F. Morse.

'A FASCINATING FILM OF THE FAR EAST' at the Arcadia Cinema, Regent Street, 1922. This cinema (which opened in 1912) was, at one time, presided over by a Mr Hook, who acted as his own one-man trailer for the next week's film. He would mount one of the front tip-up seats and tell his customers all about it himself!

STAFF ON THE ROOF of the Regent Cinema, looking west towards the GPO in Regent Circus, c. 1930. On the left: Stan Guscott (pageboy); right, -?- (chief projectionist). The false façade to the Regent was later removed. The cinema later became the Gaumont, then the Odeon and is now Top Rank Bingo.

REGENT CIRCUS in May 1930. 'Talking Pictures' have arrived at the Regent Cinema. To the right of the Cinema are the Bristol Tramways & Carriage Co. Ltd offices and the former Roman Catholic Church, then in use as a museum, on the corner.

ABC SAVOY CINEMA, Regent Street, 1952. Who would have guessed then that Ronald Reagan, star of one of the films being shown, was to be a future President of the USA? The Savoy opened in February 1937 and seated 1,170 people and is reported to have a ghost, which has been seen or heard many times since the 1940s. In later years it became the ABC, then the Cannon Cinema before closure in 1991. It is now the Savoy bar/restaurant.

THE PALACE CINEMA, Cricklade Road, c. 1957, opened in 1914 with 860 seats. Like so many other cinemas around the country it closed in the late 1950s.

THE INTERIOR OF THE PALACE CINEMA, Cricklade Road, in the 1950s.

PALLADIUM CINEMA

RODBOURNE ROAD, SWINDON.

MATINEES DAILY AT 2-30.	EVENING 6 to 10-30.
4d. and 6d.	Prices: 1/4, 1/-, 9d., 6d.

MONDAY, AUGUST 28th, for Three Days—

Another Outstanding Attraction !

Joan Bennett   Spencer Tracy

IN

PIER——13,

CERTIFICATE A.

A comedy-drama of adventure and love. . . . Full of light-hearted and bright situations. Brilliantly acted by Joan Bennett & Spencer Tracy.

ALSO

Horace Hodges   Grethe Hansen

IN

AFTER DARK, CERTIFICATE U.

SPECIAL 'U' PROGRAMME EVERY SATURDAY AFTERNOON.

Children admitted front seats, 2d.

THURSDAY, AUGUST 31st, for Three Days—

Will Rogers   Marion Nixon

IN

TOO BUSY TO WORK

CERTIFICATE U.

ALSO

THE GREAT RACING DRAMA:

Arthur Sinclair   Dodo Watts

IN

HUNDRED TO ONE

CERTIFICATE U.

AN ADVERTISING HANDBILL for the Palladium Cinema, Jennings Street, Rodbourne, 1933. This local community cinema opened in 1928 and closed in the late 1950s. The building is now used by Timeprint Ltd.

THE EMPIRE THEATRE sold, prior to demolition, in 1959.

DEMOLISHING THE EMPIRE THEATRE in 1959.

High Days and Holidays

GWR CHILDREN'S FÊTE, c. 1910. Another view of faces, young and old, at this popular annual event, first organized by the Mechanics Institution in 1868. Identified: the lady facing the camera on the left (with a child in her arms, both wearing hats) is Clara E. Beesley with daughter Nellie Emily Lydia.

A LARGE SOCIAL EVENT such as the Children's Fête required many voluntary helpers. Here we have the GWR First Aiders on duty at the Fête in 1920.

J. COMPTON & SONS LTD, clothing factory, Sheppard Street, Armistice Day 1918. Comptons were one of the main employers of female labour in Swindon for many years and supplied uniforms to the GWR. They had a contract to make uniforms for the armed services in the First World War.

KING WILLIAM STREET CHURCH OF ENGLAND SCHOOL, Peace Celebrations in 1918. The school opened in 1871, replacing the National School in Newport Street.

THE CHILDREN'S CARNIVAL at the Rink, Market Square, Old Town, in January 1911. The large hall of the Corn Exchange served as a roller-skating rink for several years prior to the First World War (see *Swindon in Old Photographs*, p. 141). The Rink later became a cinema, known throughout the district for its tenor solos in the interval. After the Second World War the hall became the Locarno Ballroom where many famous dance bands of the 1950s and 1960s performed and wrestling promotions were staged. It is now a bingo hall.

THE ORIGINAL OUTLET of Coate Water reservoir, c. 1900. Today only the top of the archway can be seen. Coate Water, built as a feeder for the Wilts & Berks Canal in 1822, has always been a favourite leisure spot for the townsfolk of Swindon.

GWR WORKS BRASS SHOP STAFF, February 1908.

GWR WORKS BRASS SHOP OUTING to Henley-on-Thames, May 1908.

GWR STORES DEPARTMENT STAFF boarding charabancs for their annual outing in June 1909 to Newton Abbot, Moretonhampstead and Becky Falls.

CROWDS IN REGENT CIRCUS awaiting the arrival of King George V and Queen Mary at the Town Hall, 28 April 1924.

THE VISIT OF KING GEORGE V AND QUEEN MARY to Swindon, 28 April 1924. The King and Queen inspected a guard of honour of ex-servicemen outside the Town Hall and spoke to the town's VC, ex-Sergeant William Gosling, before placing a wreath on the Cenotaph. After visiting the Victoria Hospital, the royal party had an hour and a half tour of the GWR Works.

THOMAS STREET, Rodbourne, during celebrations for the Jubilee of King George V and Queen Mary, 1935. The houses to the right of the picture are now Avenel Court, sheltered flats for the elderly, named after Robert and Christine Avenel, the first recorded residents of Even Swindon in the year 1313.

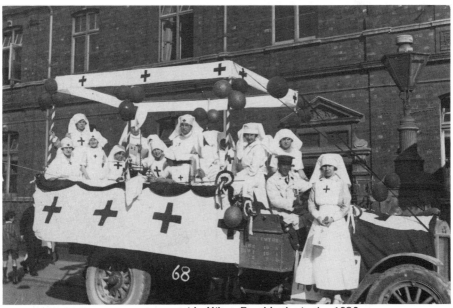

VICTORIA HOSPITAL CARNIVAL FLOAT outside Milton Road baths in the 1920s.

MARILYN CLARKE in fancy dress on the corner of Whiteman Street/Poulton Street, Gorse Hill during celebrations to mark the Coronation of Queen Elizabeth II in 1953.

From Peace into War: the Thirties and Forties

REGENT STREET, looking north, in 1930. On the left, on the corner with Havelock Street, is Anstiss' departmental store. One of the Leyland Titan low bridge buses, purchased in 1929 to replace the tramcars, is seen overtaking a vehicle parked in front of the Arcadia Cinema (see p. 105).

BRIDGE STREET, looking north in 1930. To the left is the Golden Lion public house, at the junction with the Wilts & Berks Canal site (see also p. 133).

REGENT STREET, looking south, c. 1930. Compare this photograph with that taken in 1912 on p. 42.

REGENT CIRCUS, from Princes Street, May 1930. Ahead, left, is Rolleston Street. The horse trough was still in the centre of the road at this time.

REGENT CIRCUS from Rolleston Street, May 1930. The bus is the Bristol Tramway & Carriage Co. Ltd's service to Highworth. Their buses used to park around the Town Hall for services to Chippenham, Calne, Cirencester, Marlborough, Devizes, Malmesbury, etc. These vehicles had solid tyres and travelled at a speed of 12 mph.

THE VIEW NORTH of Cheney Manor Road, from Baileys Corner (the corner of Ferndale Road) in the 1930s.

THE VIEW SOUTH down Cheney Manor Road from Rodbourne Arms in the 1930s.

A GLIMPSE INTO THE PAST – houses for £730. An advertisement for houses on the Park Farm housing estate, Marlborough Road (now Carlisle Avenue, Corby Avenue, etc.) in 1934–35.

NEWLY-BUILT HOUSES in Carlisle Avenue/Bouverie Avenue, 1936.

CORBY AVENUE, 1936. In the field in the background can be seen the big top of Bertram Mills' Circus.

LOOKING FROM CARLISLE AVENUE towards Marlborough Road, 1936. In the background are the goods transfer shed and railway sidings.

H.A. REEVES, Market Street, decorated for the Coronation of King George VI and Queen Elizabeth, May 1937. The premises are now Gran's Food Store, but the name Reeves & Co. can still be seen on the gable wall although the business closed in 1941.

FLEET STREET, YMCA and the Electricity Showroom, decorated for the Coronation of King George VI and Queen Elizabeth in 1937.

TOWN HALL, decorated and illuminated for the 1937 Coronation.

THE VIEW SOUTH UP BRIDGE STREET from the junction with Fleet Street, decorated for the 1937 Coronation.

IRON RAILINGS being removed for scrap to help the war effort, in front of H.A. Reeves hairdressing shop, 78 Commercial Road, during the Second World War. These houses were demolished in recent years for a car park near the new market.

TEN BOMBS were dropped on Beatrice and Ipswich streets during an air-raid on the night of 19/20 December 1940. Five houses were demolished and others damaged. This photograph shows demolished houses in Ipswich Street.

THE VIEW SOUTH from the junction of Ferndale Road and Whitehouse Road showing damage sustained during the raid on the night of 19/20 December 1940. Damage was caused to gas and water mains.

THE VIEW NORTH in Whitehouse Road showing bomb damage after the raid on 19/20 December 1940.

DEMOLISHED HOUSES in Beatrice Street after the air-raid on 19/20 December 1940. One person subsequently died in hospital after injuries sustained. Many had lucky escapes including several of those evacuated from London and Birmingham.

HOME GUARD GUN CREW in the Second World War at Messrs Short Bros.

THE HOME GUARD, Drill Hall, Church Place, in the Second World War.

STREET PARTY, Northampton Street, VE Day, May 1945.

SECTION NINE

After the War:
the End of an Era

THE ORIGINAL GOLDEN LION, standing in the forecourt of the Golden Lion public house by the Wilts & Berks Canal site, off Bridge Street, in 1952. Many generations of Swindon children sat on its back. When the public house was closed in 1956 the lion was destroyed by accident (see *Swindon in Old Photographs*, p. 93). The present lion in Canal Walk, by Carleton Attwood, was placed there in the Silver Jubilee Year, 1977.

THE VIEW WEST along the Wilts & Berks Canal site, across the junction with Regent and Bridge streets in 1957. The Golden Lion can just be seen over the roof of the parked car to the right.

THE SAME VIEWPOINT AS ABOVE, 1962/3. The beginnings of the new shopping precinct can be seen to the right.

MARKS & SPENCER, 85–87 Regent Street, 1945. The store was extended in 1964 by taking over the site formerly occupied by the Fox Tavern on the corner of Cromwell Street.

MORSE'S DEPARTMENTAL STORE at 10/12 Regent Street, in the 1950s; the large shop belonging to the Morse family of the Croft, Old Town. W.H. Smith's store now stands on this site.

REGENT STREET, looking south, c. 1950. The Eagle hotel to the left, on the corner of College Street, was closed in the early 1950s. The Works bookshop now occupies this site.

CROMWELL STREET, looking west from Regent Street, November 1963. To the left is the wall of the Fox Tavern, demolished shortly afterwards for the extension to Marks & Spencer's store. To the right is the Connaught Restaurant, where many Swindonians used to enjoy a meal.

THE VIEW TO REGENT STREET, from Havelock Street, c. 1962. McIlroy's store is to the right with the entrance to the ballroom where regular Saturday night dances were held and traditional jazz club meetings. Many well-known pop groups also played there, including the Beatles on 17 July 1962 !

REGENT STREET, looking south, c. 1964. The Arcadia Cinema was then the Classic Cartoon Cinema.

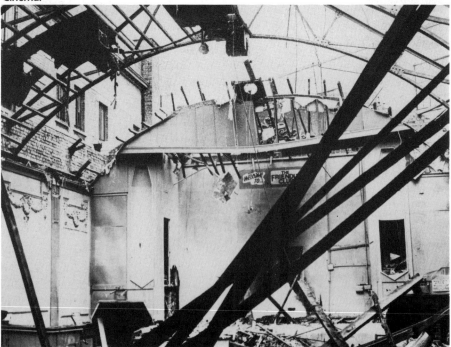

THE FORMER ARCADIA CINEMA in Regent Street during demolition in August 1974.

A MARCH AGAINST REDUNDANCY in Commercial Road, Swindon, in the early 1960s. Men from Pressed Steel, British Railways, Plesseys and Vickers Armstrong joined the demonstration. It was the beginning of the many cut-backs in industrial employment over the next two decades. Note the old Market to the left.

COMMERCIAL ROAD, December 1968, looking west.

CLACK'S CORNER STORES, Curtis Street, with the Central Club in Milton Road to the right in 1968.

THE FORMER CENTRAL CLUB AND INSTITUTE, Milton Road, in 1968. It was built adjacent to the Wilts & Berks Canal in 1897. This building was demolished in the 1970s after being used as a discotheque for some years and also a temporary magistrates' court.

THE JUNCTION (LEFT) OF GORDON ROAD AND PRINCES STREET, c. 1960. The road ahead is crossing Whale Bridge with the Whale public house and H.C. Preater's Garage to the right. Cowies Garage (formerly Walker Jackson's) now stands on the site of Preater's.

CORPORATION STREET, the view towards Whale Bridge, showing the off-licence to the right on the corner of Oriel Street, September 1960.

PRINCES STREET, looking south towards the Town Hall, August 1970.

PROVIDENCE ROW, Regents Place, c. 1960. Regents Place, Cow Lane and the original Red Cow public house stood near the site of Wyvern Theatre Square and the Courts car park.

More Country Lanes and Surrounding Villages

THE PLOUGH INN, Badbury, Chiseldon, 1906. Charles Moore, landlord, is on the right.

MARLBOROUGH ROAD looking east, c. 1928. To the right is the Polo House which stood on the corner of the Polo Field.

DROVE ROAD, summer 1905.

DROVE ROAD, April 1908.

MOREDON ROAD. Maundrells Farm was on the left and the Red Lion public house opposite it on the right on the corner of The Street, leading down to Haydon Wick, c. 1910.

BLUNSDON HILL, looking north, in the 1920s.

BLUNSDON ABBEY, c. 1890. A magnificent building in the Neo-Gothic style, it was built in 1864 for Clayton de Windt, a wealthy sportsman. The designs were by E. Mantell of London and the builder was Thomas Barrett of Swindon. It was considered to be one of the finest houses in the west of England and was lavishly furnished. A view from the church.

BLUNSDON ABBEY, C. 1890. A view from the lake.

BLUNSDON ABBEY FIRE, 22 April 1904. The Swindon Fire Brigade, under Captain Pritchett and Deputy-Captain Mundy, attempted in vain to put out the blaze, pumping water from the adjacent lake. Occupants of the house were rescued by jumping into blankets from the bedroom windows. Unfortunately the house was completely destroyed. Only some of the external walls remain today and the site is now occupied by Blunsdon Abbey Caravans Ltd.

THE MEET OF THE VALE OF THE WHITE HORSE HOUNDS near Cold Harbour Inn, Blunsdon, 1892. The inn was rebuilt in 1894.

A DECORATED WAGON on Hospital Fête Saturday, Blunsdon, c. 1905.

BLUNSDON CHURCH SCHOOL, c. 1890. Built in the mid-1800s it eventually became a National School.

BLUNSDON SCHOOL, c. 1905. The school was enlarged shortly after the turn of the century.

FARMWORKERS at Blunsdon in 1900. The old farmhouse in the background was then the home of the Hunt-Titcombe family.

THE MEET OF THE FOXHOUNDS, Wanborough Village, 1906.

A SUNDAY SCHOOL OUTING at Hinton Parva, near Swindon, 1913.

NINE ELMS, Shaw, c. 1910, when this was a quiet country hamlet.

LOADING MILK CHURNS at Stratton station, on the GWR Highworth Branch line in the 1920s. Numerous farms sent their milk here to be forwarded to London each day. These 17-gallon churns were extremely heavy to manoeuvre and were later replaced by 10-gallon containers. The line was finally closed in 1962.

ERMIN STREET, Stratton St Margaret, looking north, 1912. To the right is the willow tree planted ceremonially in 1900 to replace a very old tree blown down in a gale at the turn of the century. The new tree did not survive past the 1920s but a lime tree, planted nearby, survives to this day despite the impact of an aircraft which crashed into it during the Second World War.

THE 'NEW' ST PHILIP'S CHURCH, Upper Stratton, in 1904. The chancel of the church was not built for another six years and, internally, the parishioners faced a large brick wall until the chancel was built.

SOUTH MARSTON VICARAGE, 1910. Now a hotel and country club.

SOUTH MARSTON CHURCH CHOIR on an outing to the South Coast, c. 1912. The Vicar, the Revd Angus Macdonald (bearded) is in the centre of the back row.

WILLIAM MAISEY, farmer at South Marston, 1914.

JANE, daughter of William Maisey.

ALFRED WILLIAMS, 'The Hammerman Poet' of South Marston, while in the Royal Field Artillery in India, 1917–18.

SOUTH MARSTON VILLAGE, c. 1905. In the centre is Cambria Cottage, birthplace of Alfred Williams and, on the right, Dryden Cottage, where he lived for several years after his marriage.

A SCHOOL GROUP at South Marston in the 1880s.

SOUTH MARSTON SCHOOLBOYS digging the schoolhouse garden for educational purposes, we presume. Miss Cross, the Schoolmistress, views their labours in 1912.

ACKNOWLEDGEMENTS

The Swindon Society would like to thank all those listed below for their assistance in the compilation of this book. Especially Society members Mrs Jean Allen, Denis Bird and Brian Bridgeman, who undertook the task of putting the book together and selecting the photographs to be used. Also to Denis, Richard and Lydia Clarke, Colin Herbert, Keith Saunders and Tony Daglish for providing various photographs from their collections and Denis again for several from his own camera taken around the town since the early 1950s. The Society would also like to thank all those members and friends who have supplied photographs or information and Bill Brettell for allowing us to use some extracts from his notes about old Swindon in the Introduction. Unfortunately, again, not all photographs supplied could be used due to space restrictions.

Our thanks are also due to the Borough of Thamesdown Museum Service, to the staff of Swindon Reference Library (Wiltshire Library and Museum Service), Mr David Marchant of Ridgeway Studios; Mr John Mayhew, Editor of the *Evening Advertiser*; Mr L.A. Thompson of the AEU; Mr D.A. Moss of Bradley Homes; British Railways Board; and Lens of Sutton. Also former Swindon Society secretary, David Luker, who originally obtained many of the photographs in the Society Collection.

For individual contributions the Society would also like to thank:
Mrs J. Allen • Mr F. Avenell • Mr D. Backhouse • Mr D. Barrett • Mr A. Bizley
Mr W.A. Brettell • Mr B. Bridgeman • Mr T. Browne • Mrs M. Clack
the late Miss M.F. Crowdy • Lorna Davies • Mr M. Fox • Mr F. French
The Revd F.W.T. Fuller • Mr J. Gould • Mr J. Hacker • Mr R. Hunt
Mr S.J. Jones • Miss M. Kynaston • D. Lacey • Mr J. Lawrence
Mr J. Maisey JP • Mrs B. MacDonald • Mr & Mrs C.W. McLeod
Mrs M. Philpin • Mr P.S.A. Redmond • Mr K. Robertson
The Very Revd R.J. Twomey • Mrs M. Townsend • Mr M. Vandervelde
Miss J. Walker • Mr G. Weare • Mr K. Weeks • Mr G. Wirdnam.

Doubts exist regarding the original source of some photographs used in this book, many of which have been in the Society Collection for a large number of years, and the Swindon Society apologizes for any omissions from the list of names given above.